The Key to English

A guide for GCSE and Standard Grade

Malcolm Young

Solomon
Press

Published by Solomon Press
Unit1, Rydon Farm,
West Newton, Somerset, TA7 0BZ

Tel: 0700 900 1548 or 0709 100 1548
E-mail: info@solomon-press.com

Web site: www.solomon-press.com

© Malcolm Young 2000
First published 2000

ISBN 1 901724 13 1

Design and typesetting by Pedeke Ltd. Bridgwater, Somerset.
Printed by The Friary Press, Dorchester, Dorset.

Contents

Foreword

In this Guide I have tried to include, in as few pages as possible and in the simplest of language, everything the GCSE and Standard Grade student could be expected to know in the areas of English grammar, punctuation and spelling. Clear, unambiguous written English will, of course, stand you in good stead in any examination but I have also included a section on Figures of Speech and Literary Devices which is more specific to the subjects of English Language and Literature.

One way to use this Guide is to start with the Glossary near the back of the book. Let us say that, for example, you have a query about Pronouns.

1 Look up **Pronoun** in the Glossary, which is in alphabetical order. You will find a brief definition and it will direct you to *Study p.17*.

2 *Pages 17* and *18* will tell you everything you need to know about the seven different kinds of pronouns.

3 When you have studied those pages you will be directed to *Tests 6 and 7*, on pages 54 and 55.

4 The answers are at the back of the book. Mark your work very carefully because this can form the most valuable part of the whole learning process. If, for any reason, you are dissatisfied with the result of your test, go back and spend a little more time on the study pages.

Alternatively, you may find it useful to work through the book methodically, starting with the Grammar Section and completing the tests as you go.

The ability to express oneself clearly and confidently has much to do with success in English and most other subjects, as well as in many other areas of life, and it is with that in mind that I have compiled this book. I hope that you will find it of use, and finally I wish you every success in your own examinations.

Malcolm Young

Grammar

THE SENTENCE

What is a sentence?

A simple enough question but the answer may not be quite so easy.

A sentence starts with a capital letter and ends with a full stop (or a question mark or exclamation mark). Well that certainly describes a written sentence but does not define it.

A sentence is a complete thought in words. That is a closer definition.

A sentence is a group of words arranged in such a way that they express a complete thought. It can stand alone and needs no other words to help it. If we accept this as a definition we can move on to look at the various types of sentence that exist.

There are four main types of sentence: **statement**, **imperative** (command), **interrogative** and **exclamatory**.

A **statement sentence** conveys information.

> EXAMPLE: *The dog stole the meat.*
> *The Martins, who live in number 33, have recently bought a new caravan and parked it on their front lawn.*

An **imperative sentence** requests or commands action.

> EXAMPLE: *Please sit down.*
> *Take this note to the Head and wait for a reply.*

An **interrogative sentence** requests information.

> EXAMPLE: *Where is the cat?*
> *Have you bought the fruit or do you want me to get it?*

An **exclamatory sentence** usually expresses feelings or is said loudly, with surprise or as a warning.

> EXAMPLE: *How lovely to see you!*
> *Look out!*
> *What a marvellous surprise!*

In all the examples given above it should be noticed that some sentences are **simple** (conveying a single thought) while others have added other bits of information: these are called **complex** sentences.

To write or speak correct English you should know how the various words within a sentence function. According to their function these words are called **nouns**, **verbs**, **adjectives**, **adverbs**, **pronouns**, **conjunctions**, **prepositions** or **interjections**.

NOUNS

The name of a person, animal, place or thing.
There are various types of noun: **common**, **proper**, **collective**, **abstract**, **singular**, **plural**, **masculine** and **feminine**.

A **common noun** is the name of a general (not specific) person, animal, place or thing;
    EXAMPLE: *girl, squirrel, village, knife.*

A **proper noun** is the name of a specific person, animal, place or thing.
A proper noun always starts with a capital letter.
    EXAMPLE: *John Brown, a Clydesdale Horse, a King Charles Spaniel,*
               Scotland, The Daily Express.

A **collective noun** is the name of special group of people or animals.
    EXAMPLE: *choir* (of singers), *herd* (of cattle), *school* (of whales)
              team (of players).

An **abstract noun** is the name given to something which has no material existence.
    EXAMPLE: *beauty, excitement, anxiety, success.*
             (Nouns with material existence are called **concrete nouns**.)

Singular nouns may sound simple enough but there is a difficulty which can occur when using collective nouns (above). Although a *herd* of cattle is obviously referring to more than one animal, the collective noun *herd* should be treated as a singular noun.
    EXAMPLE: *A herd of cattle is grazing in the meadow.*
             The team lost its first three matches.

Plural nouns (more than one) can create difficulties in spelling.
If in doubt refer to the Spelling Section of this guide which starts with "Four Rules for Changing Singular Nouns to Plural."

There are some nouns which are always used as plural.
    EXAMPLE: *scissors, trousers, jeans, pyjamas, tights.*

Gender is worth a mention at this stage.

There are four genders in English Grammar:
  Masculine (nouns used specifically for male persons or animals)
  EXAMPLE: *husband, gander, king, landlord,*
  Feminine (for female persons or animals)
  EXAMPLE: *princess, actress, doe, landlady,*
  Common (for words which can refer to either sex)
  EXAMPLE: *child, nurse, cat, receptionist,*
  Neuter (for words which refer to neither sex)
  EXAMPLE: *book, computer, photograph, view.*   *Test Yourself 1 p.49*

VERBS

A verb is frequently defined as "a doing word" or "a being word".
The verb is the most important word (or group of words) in a sentence because without it that sentence would not make sense.

The infinitive: This is the name we give to that form of the verb which is its starting point, out of which all other forms of the verb come.
It starts with the word *to* so that the infinitive of verbs are *to hide, to run, to shout, to hope, to think.*

It was once thought to be very poor English to split the infinitive. This is when an adverb is placed in the middle of the infinitive form of the verb.
  EXAMPLE: *to boldly go, to clearly see.*

Nowadays the ruling is not so strict but it is as well to know that *to go boldly*, or *to see clearly* are still generally considered to be better.

Transitive and intransitive verbs: All sentences have a subject and a verb.
The subject is the person, thing or place (noun or pronoun) that does the action of the verb.
  EXAMPLE: *Jack shouts.*

This little sentence is about *Jack* (subject) and what he does – *shouts* (verb).

Many sentences also have an **object**. This is the person, place or thing (noun or pronoun) that has the action of the verb done to it.
  EXAMPLE: *The dog bit Mary.*

This sentence is about *The dog* (subject), what it did – *bit* (verb), and who had the action done to her – *Mary* (object).

Verbs that take an object are called **transitive**; verbs that do not take an object are called **intransitive**.

Agreement: a verb has to agree with its subject in person and number.
If the subject is singular the verb has to take the singular form.
If the subject is plural, the verb has to be plural.

Person: (printed here as a point of reference.)

1st person singular	=	*I*
2nd person singular	=	*you*
3rd person singular	=	*he, she* or *it*
1st person plural	=	*we*
2nd person plural	=	*you*
3rd person plural	=	*they*

Auxiliary verbs: the verbs *to be, to have, to do* are all verbs in their own right (*I **am** a carpenter. A spider **has** eight legs. We **did** the work.*) but they can also serve as auxiliary or helping verbs when used with other verbs.

EXAMPLE: *I **am** hoping, she **was** speaking, they **had** caught, he **has** opened, we **did** insist.*

In this way a verb may consist of more than one word.

Other auxiliary verbs include: *can, could, may, might, must, would, should, will, shall* – all necessary when forming the different tenses of verbs.

Test Yourself 3 (q.1) p.51

Negative verbs: these are formed by adding *not* after the auxiliary verb.

EXAMPLE: *have opened* becomes *have **not** opened*, *can see* becomes *can**not** see.*

Where there are more than one auxiliary *not* usually comes after the first auxiliary.

EXAMPLE: *I should have gone* becomes *I should **not** have gone* rather than *I should have **not** gone.*

Participles: this is the name given to two forms of the verb – the **present participle** and the **past participle**.

In regular verbs the present participle is formed by adding *-ing* to the infinitive of the verb.

EXAMPLE: *shout – shouting, look – looking, jump – jumping.*

In regular verbs the past participle is formed by adding -ed to the infinitive of the verb.

EXAMPLE: *shout – shouted, look – looked, jump – jumped.*

Regular and irregular verbs: most verbs in the English language follow the rules outlined above to form the past participle. However, there are quite a number that do not and these are called **irregular verbs**.

Here is a list of a few irregular verbs but there are many more:

Infinitive	Past tense	Past Participle
to blow	blew	blown
to break	broke	broken
to catch	caught	caught
to draw	drew	drawn
to eat	ate	eaten
to fly	flew	flown
to grow	grew	grown
to have	had	had
to know	knew	known
to lie	lay	lain
to make	made	made
to ring	rang	rung
to spring	sprang	sprung
to tear	tore	torn
to write	wrote	written

Test Yourself 3 (q.2) p.51

Active and Passive verbs. A verb may be described as being in the Active Voice or the Passive Voice.

In **Transitive** and **Intransitive verbs** (above) we discussed the functions of subject, verb and object within a simple sentence.
When the subject carries out the action of the verb (*The dog bit Mary.*) the verb is said to be in the active voice. Here there is a transfer of the action from the subject (*The dog*) to the object (*Mary*).
However, the sentence could read *Mary was bitten by the dog.*
The meaning is the same but now *Mary* has become the subject of the sentence but instead of carrying out the action of the verb she is having the action done to her.
This form of the verb is called the **passive voice**.

The following examples should make it clear:

Active Voice	Passive Voice
John is cleaning the floors.	The floors are being cleaned by John.
I will open the shop.	The shop will be opened by me.
The English defeated the Scots.	The Scots were defeated by the English.
The Council do not allow cycling.	Cycling is not allowed.

Test Yourself 2 (q.3) p50

The interrogative form of the verb.

This is the form used to ask questions and is formed by changing the order.

> EXAMPLE: *Alice* (subject) *was* (auxiliary) *annoying* (main verb) *Harry.* (object)
> This becomes:
> *Was* (auxiliary) *Alice* (subject) *annoying* (main verb) *Harry?* (object)

The imperative form of the verb.

This is the form used for commands or requests and it is formed from the second person form (*you*) by leaving off the word *you*.

> EXAMPLE: *You stop it!* becomes *Stop it!*
> *You follow the rest!* becomes *Follow the rest!*
> *You excuse me.* becomes *Excuse me.*

Tenses of verbs.

The tense of a verb is the form it takes to show the time at which the action takes place.

In simplest terms it may refer to the present (now), the past (time gone by) or the future (time to come).

It may be helpful to take a simple, regular verb like *to travel* and show the various tenses in which it may be used, for example in the third person singular:

Present Simple:	*she travels*
Past Simple:	*she travelled*
Future Simple:	*she will travel*

Within these time zones it is possible to use what are called the continuous tenses:

Present Continuous:	*she is travelling*
Past Continuous:	*she was travelling*
Future Continuous:	*she will be travelling*

The perfect tense tells us about actions just completed in the present, past or future.

Present Perfect: *she has travelled*
Past Perfect (a.k.a. Pluperfect) : *she had travelled*
Future Perfect: *she will have travelled*

The perfect continuous tense tells us about actions which may be finished or not finished.

Present Perfect Continuous: *she has been travelling*
Past Perfect Continuous: *she had been travelling*
Future Perfect Continuous: *she will have been travelling*

It is a fairly common error to change tenses when writing and this can be confusing for the reader. When you are writing you should establish firmly in your mind when the action is taking place and keep to that time zone throughout the piece. *Test Yourself 2 (q.2) p.50*

Phrasal verbs.
Many verbs are made up of a simple verb followed by a preposition or adverb such as *on, off, up, through, in.*
Sometimes the two words really are verb + preposition/adverb as below:

> *The hook was designed <u>to hang on</u> the branch.*
> *Please <u>break off</u> a piece for me.*
> *She <u>called up</u> the stairs.*
> *They <u>fell through</u> the ceiling.*
> *He was invited <u>to bring in</u> his dog.*

However, these verb combinations can be used in different ways which makes them phrasal verbs, as in these sentences:

> *Please <u>hang on</u> for a few more minutes.*
> *Sadly they <u>broke off</u> negotiations.*
> *Because of lack of interest the event <u>fell through</u>.*
> *The Minister was responsible for <u>bringing in</u> a new law.*

There are many more of these phrasal verbs including: *carry out, let down, pass off, get by, check up, take in, wear off, show up, run down, ring up.*
Test Yourself 3 (q.3) p.51

ADJECTIVES

An adjective is a describing word, used to tell us more about a noun or a pronoun.

Descriptive adjectives (answering the question *What kind of?*) are also called Adjectives of quality.
> EXAMPLE: *A **small** bird, his **quick** response, my **elderly** aunt, **poor** Angie.*

The adjectives in those four simple examples come before the nouns they describe but they do not always need to and there may be more than one.
> EXAMPLE: *Michael was **cold** and **hungry**. The sea was **rough** and **icy**.*
> ***Dear, old, lovable** Henry is **happy** today.*
> *The **ancient, blue** bus will be **slow**.*

Possessive adjectives tell us who the owner of a noun is, answering the question *Whose?*
They include the words: *my, your, his, her, its, our, your* (plural), *their.*

Adjectives of quantity tell us the number or amount, answering the questions *How many?* or *How much?*
> EXAMPLE: *All the numbers plus words like sixth, seventh, many, most, much, few, several, enough, little, less.*

Proper adjectives are formed from proper nouns and start with a capital.
> EXAMPLE: *English, German, Islamic, Christian, Georgian, Elizabethan, Biblical.*

Demonstrative adjectives are used to distinguish and answer the questions *Which?* or *What?*
They include the words *this, that, these, those* but they must always be linked to a noun.
> EXAMPLE: ***Which** book? – **This** book. **Which** houses? – **Those** houses.*

(Take care not to confuse the four demonstrative adjectives with pronouns. Demonstrative pronouns are the same words but used in a stand-alone context.)
> Example ***This** is exciting. You'd be better off with **those**.*

Interrogative adjectives are used to ask questions: *Which? What? Whose?*
Like the demonstrative adjectives above these must also be used with nouns or they become pronouns.
> EXAMPLE: ***Which** tie do you prefer? **What** colour are you painting the wall? **Whose** coat is this?*

Distributive adjectives

These are used to refer to individual members of a class or group and include the words *each, every, either, neither,* but again need to be used with a noun.

    EXAMPLE: **every** *pupil,* **each** *representative,* **either** *programme.*

Order of adjectives.

When using more than one adjective with a noun or pronoun there is an accepted order in which the adjectives should be placed.
It is: *opinion – size – age – shape – colour – origin – material – purpose. (O-S-A-S-C-O-M-P)*

    EXAMPLE: **yellow, French, every-day** *china (colour – origin – purpose)*
           a **beautiful, old, wooden** *doll (opinion – age – material)*

Adjectives: comparatives and superlatives.

The comparative is used to compare two nouns.
As a general rule adjectives of one syllable add *-er* to form the comparative.

    EXAMPLE: *tall – taller, bright – brighter, loud – louder.*

Adjectives of more than one syllable are preceded by the word more to form the comparative.

    EXAMPLE: *beautiful – more beautiful, exciting – more exciting,*
           wonderful – more wonderful.

The superlative is used when more than two nouns are compared.
As a general rule adjectives of more than one syllable add *-est* to form the superlative, while those with more than one syllable are preceded by the word *most.*

    EXAMPLE: *tallest, brightest, loudest, most beautiful, most exciting,*
           most wonderful.

Adjectives and their endings.

It is helpful to know that adjectives ending in *-ing* usually describe what something is like, while adjectives ending in *-ed* usually describe people's feelings.

    EXAMPLE: *This was a surprising ending.*
           There was a surprised look on his face.

           She was a very frightened child.
           It was a very frightening experience.

           The language sounded confusing.
           The confused passengers left the train.

Adjectival phrases.

An adjectival phrase is a group of words that does the work of a single adjective.

Instead of: *Homeless people were sleeping on park benches.* (adjectives) we may write:

People without any homes were sleeping on benches in the park. (adjectival phrases).

Test Yourself 4 p.52

ADVERBS

In the same way as adjectives are used to tell us more about nouns and pronouns, adverbs are used to tell us more about any other words in a sentence – mainly verbs, adjectives and other adverbs.

Adverbs answer the questions:

How?	Adverb of *manner*
When?	Adverb of *time*
Where?	Adverb of *place*
How much?	Adverb of *degree*
How often?	Adverb of *number or frequency*
How likely?	Adverb of *probability*

There are also **interrogative** and **relative adverbs**.
The eight kinds of adverbs are dealt with below.

Adverbs of manner.

These are the most common kind of adverbs and they tell us *how* something happens.

Most adverbs of manner are formed from adjectives by adding -*ly*.

EXAMPLE: *happy - happily, beautiful – beautifully, slow – slowly.*

Adverbs of time.

These tell us *when* something happens and they include words like *tomorrow, soon, later, tomorrow, earlier, since, now, afterwards, then.*

Adverbs of place.

These tell us *where* something happens and they include words like *here, there, upstairs, downstairs, outdoors, indoors, nowhere, everywhere,* … and many others.

Adverbs of degree.

These tell us *how much* or *by how much* something happens and include words such as *quite, almost, much, only, rather, hardly, too, very.* Mostly those words listed here will be used to tell us about verbs but sometimes adverbs of degree are used to modify an adjective or another adverb.

EXAMPLE: *The soup was **too** hot.* (*too* is an adverb of degree telling us about an adjective). *They played **quite** happily.* (*quite* is an adverb of degree telling us about an adverb)

Adverbs of number or frequency.

These are used to tell us *how often* something happens and include words like *once, twice, sometimes, never, usually, always.*

Adverbs of probability.

They tell us *how sure* we are of something and include *perhaps, probably, definitely, certainly.* We may also include here the words *yes* and *no* although some people would call these **adverbs of affirmation** and **negation**.

EXAMPLE: *The train will **probably** be late.*
***Yes**, I can **certainly** be there.*

Interrogative adverbs.

These are used to ask questions and include, *How? Where? When? Why?*

EXAMPLE: ***How** will you find it?*
***Where** did you lose it?*
***When** did you last have it?*
***Why** were you not more careful?*

Relative adverbs.

These include the same words as interrogative adverbs (above) but here they are used in sentences that are not asking questions.

EXAMPLE: *He did not know **how** he would find it.*
*He could not think **where** he had lost it.*
*He remembered **when** he had last used it.*

Adverbial phrases.

These are made up of more than one word.

EXAMPLE: *We will meet **by chance**.*   *manner*
*We will meet **under the clock**.*   *place*
*We will meet **before very long**.*   *time*
*We will meet **three times a week**.*   *frequency*

Position of adverbs.
Adverbs can appear at the beginning, middle or end of a sentence.
EXAMPLE: *Then the dog **suddenly** started to growl **fiercely**.*

There are six rules about the position of adverbs:

* **Adverbs of manner** usually go in the middle or at the end of a sentence.
  EXAMPLE: *She **slowly** fell asleep. She fell asleep **slowly**.*

* **Adverbs of place and time** usually go at the end of sentences.
  EXAMPLE: *There is a swimming pool **nearby**. We arrived **early**.*

* **Single word adverbs of frequency** usually go in the middle but may be
  more effective at the beginning when used for emphasis.
  EXAMPLE: *The fair **usually** comes in May. **Usually** the fair comes in May.*

  However, **adverbial phrases of frequency** may be better at the end.
  EXAMPLE: *The baker calls **three times a week**.*

* When using the verb *to be* the adverb comes after it.
  EXAMPLE: *Martin **is always** happy. The boys **were obviously** guilty.*

* An adverb does not usually go between the verb and its direct object.
  EXAMPLE: *Liz opened **quickly** her parcel.* (Sounds awkward, doesn't it?)
  *Liz opened her parcel **quickly**.* (That's better!)

* When there is more than one adverb in a sentence, the usual order is:
  manner – place – time (although there will be times when, for the sake of
  emphasis, you will not want to follow this order.)
  EXAMPLE: *They met **by accident*** (manner) ***in the park*** (place) ***one
  afternoon*** (time).

Adverbs – comparative and superlative.
In the same way as adjectives are used to compare nouns and pronouns,
adverbs may be used to compare actions.
The **comparative form** is used to compare two actions while the **superlative**
is used when there are more than two.
General rule: adverbs of one syllable add *-er, -est. hard, harder, hardest.*
However, most adverbs have more than one syllable and for these, as a
general rule, use *more ... , most ...*
EXAMPLE: *quickly, more quickly, most quickly.*

Test Yourself 5 p.53

PRONOUNS

A **pronoun** is a word used instead of a noun. That sounds simple but in fact there is much to say about pronouns because there are seven different kinds.

Personal pronouns.
These vary depending on whether they are the subject or the object of a sentence.

Subject form: *I you(s) he she it we you*(pl) *they.*
Object form: *me you him her it us you them.*

In comparisons we should always use the object form of the pronoun.
EXAMPLE: *You are not as clever as **me**. I am older than **him**.*

Some books of grammar will tell you (quite correctly) that the verb *to be* should always be followed by subject pronouns.
EXAMPLE: *It is **I**. It was **they**. It is **she**.*

Today we tend to say *"It is me." "It is them." "It is her."* .This is becoming accepted English by usage. The more correct forms sound stilted.

Possessive pronouns.
These are used without nouns to show ownership.
They are: *mine, yours, his, hers, its, ours, yours, theirs.*
EXAMPLE: *This is **my** book.* becomes *This is **mine**.*

Reflexive pronouns.
These are used to refer back to a noun or pronoun in a sentence. They are: *myself, yourself, himself, herself, itself, ourselves, yourselves, themselves.*
EXAMPLE: *Jane was talking to **herself**. I did the whole thing **myself**.*
*We cooked the meal **ourselves**.*

Interrogative pronouns.
Who? Whom? Whose? Which? What? Interrogative pronouns stand in for nouns in sentences that ask questions. Use *Who? Whom? Whose?* for people; use *Which? What?* for things. *Who?* is the subject form.
EXAMPLE: ***Who** would like an ice-cream?*

Whom? is the object form.
EXAMPLE: *To **whom** shall I send this card?*

Whose? can sometimes be confused with the adjective.
EXAMPLE: ***Whose** is this?* (**pronoun** - it is used instead of a noun)
***Whose** coat is this?* (**adjective** - used with a noun to describe it)

Relative pronouns. *who, whom, whose, which, that.*

Notice they are almost the same words as the interrogative pronouns (above) but as relative pronouns they are used to relate one part of a sentence to another by standing in for a noun already used.

Use *who, whom, whose* for people, *which* and *that* for things.

Who is the subject form; *whom* is the object form.

> EXAMPLE: *Have you met Lucy **who** lives in Station Road?*
> *Jenny, **for whom** we have collected, will be fifty next week.*
> *Stan is a lorry driver **whose** work takes him to France.*
> *Here is the castle **which** was lived in by Lord Percy.*
> *Did you receive the letter **that** I sent to you?*

Demonstrative pronouns. *this, that, these, those.*

These are used to point out (or demonstrate) something where the noun is understood. As with the interrogative pronouns (above) take care not to confuse the demonstrative pronoun with a demonstrative adjective.

> EXAMPLE: ***This** is exciting.* (**pronoun** because it is used instead of a noun)
> ***This** book is exciting.* (**adjective** - with a noun to describe it).

Indefinite pronouns.

These are used to take the place of unspecified persons, places and things. They include words such as *one, none, any, other, some.*

When used with nouns these words are adjectives (*one* cat, the *other* person, *some* bread) but they become indefinite pronouns when they stand alone.

> EXAMPLE: *Would you like **one**?*
> *I have lost the **other**.*
> *There is **some** left.*

Other pronouns that are used in this way include *any, each, either, neither, few, several, no-one, nobody, anybody, somebody, much, more, most*

Singular indefinite pronouns must not be treated as plurals.

> EXAMPLE: *Everyone should carry **their** own luggage.*   (incorrect)
> *Everyone should carry **his (or her)** own luggage.* (correct)

Singular indefinite pronouns should take singular verb forms.

> EXAMPLE: *None of the children **have** been left behind.*   (incorrect)
> *None (meaning not one) **has** been left behind.* (correct)

Test Yourself 6 and 7 pp. 54/55

CONJUNCTIONS

These are words used to join. We use **conjunctions** to join together single words: two nouns – *bread and butter*; two adjectives – *black or white, naughty but nice*; two adverbs – *slowly but surely*; two pronouns – *you before me*; two verbs – *run and jump*.

Conjunctions may also join phrases: *red roses or blue violets, going shopping before having lunch.* They are used to link together clauses and simple sentences in order to build longer and more interesting ones. We call these **complex sentences**.

Simple conjunctions include: *and, or, but, so, because, since, although, unless, when, while, before, after, where, whereas, as, if, yet, whenever, wherever, despite.*

Conjunctions may consist of more than one word: *as soon as, in order that, as well as, as far as, as if, provided that, in spite of.*

Conjunctions may also be used in pairs: *either... or, neither... nor, not only... but also, so... that.*
Test Yourself 8 (q.1/2/5) p.56

PREPOSITIONS

These are words which usually give us some meaning of position, time or direction. They include: *to, at, before, after, since, on, off, under, beneath, above, against, until, near, with, without, of, across, for, from, over, around, by, along, between, among, opposite, below, through, beside, up in, into.*

Compound prepositions include: *out of, next to, in front of, as well as, at the side of, in addition to, because of, instead of, according to.*

Take care not to confuse **prepositions** with **adverbs**.
The difference is simple: a preposition must be followed by something but an adverb may just relate to its verb.
The chair fell over. (adverb) *The cow jumped over the moon.* (preposition)
The cat climbed through. (adverb.) *The man ran through the door.* (preposition)
Test Yourself 8 (q.3/4/5) p.56

INTERJECTIONS

These are the simplest of all parts of speech – words which express exclamation or an emotional noise.
EXAMPLE: *Oh! Sh! Ouch! Help! Whew! Look out!*

They are usually used with exclamation marks.

Punctuation

When we speak to each other we use pauses and emphasis to make our meaning clear. When we write we need punctuation to serve the same purpose – to avoid ambiguity and leave our reader in no doubt about the precise meaning of what we have written. That is all Punctuation is – a series of marks that, if we all use them in the same way, will avoid confusion and misunderstanding.

In this section of the Guide the following punctuation topics are dealt with:

Capital Letters	Inverted Commas
Full Stop	Colon
Exclamation Mark	Semi-colon
Question Mark	Brackets
Comma	Dash
Apostrophe	Hyphen
Quotation Marks	Ellipsis

Study carefully any of the above topics about which you have any doubts. Then test yourself by completing the exercises in the "Test Your Punctuation" pages that follow.

CAPITAL LETTERS

Although the capital letter is, strictly speaking, not a punctuation mark, it is dealt with here because of its importance to the rest of the subject. There follow 12 uses of the capital letter.

1 Every sentence should start with a Capital Letter. This is not difficult to remember but it is surprising how often the capital letter is missed when the sentence is within another sentence as in Direct Speech.
   EXAMPLE: *The ship is sinking.* (Easy!) *She screamed, "The ship is sinking."* This is where a mistake can easily occur.

2 Proper nouns should always start with a Capital Letter, without exception.
   Many people remember to use capitals for names such as *John* and *Susan* but think that nicknames such as *Chalky* and *Speedy* or the names of animals like *Patch* and *Pooch* do not need capitals. They do!

3 Capital letters are also needed for people's titles like *Mr, Mrs, Miss, Dr., Lady Wilkins, Lord Pilkington, Her Royal Highness.*

4 The names of towns, villages, cities, counties, countries, rivers, mountains, particular buildings such as *Yeovil, Long Compton, Glasgow, Sussex, Wales, River Thames, Mount Everest, Holyrood Palace.*

5 Points of the compass do not use capital letters (*north, south, western, easterly*) but when used in place names such as *West Glamorgan, Northern Ireland*, they do.

6 Adjectives which are formed from proper nouns should have capital letters. For example *Ireland - Irish, Elizabeth - Elizabethan.*

7 The pronoun *I* is always written as a capital and there is no exception, though for some unknown reason *me* and *myself* do not require capitals.

8 Days of the week and months of the year have capital letters (*Monday, Friday, March, December*) but for some unknown reason, the seasons of the year (*spring, summer*) do not need them.

9 Books, plays, films, television programmes, newspapers, magazines etc. all use capital letters: *'Black Beauty', 'A Midsummer Night's Dream', 'Coronation Street', 'The Daily Mirror', 'Teen Scene'.*
   However, not every word in a title need have a capital; small words are excepted as in *'The Cricket on the Hearth'.*

10 Names of organisations, political parties, religions follow the same pattern as the books above: *The Royal Society for the Prevention of Cruelty to Animals, The Liberal Party, Hinduism and Christianity.*

11 It follows naturally that capitals will be used for:
   • abbreviations (*R.S.P.C.A., B.B.C.*)
   • initials (*G.B.Shaw, D.H.Lawrence*)
   • acronyms (*NATO, UNICEF, AIDS*).

12 In poetry it is the custom to identify the beginning of each new line by using a capital letter, although in some modern verse this practice has been abandoned.

FULL STOP

This is the first and most basic punctuation mark it is used to show the reader that the sentence has ended unless we divide our writing into sentences all kinds of unnecessary confusion and misunderstanding will inevitably occur hopefully we can all agree on when it should be used

1 A full stop is used at the end of a statement sentence.
   The sentence may:
   contain a transitive verb, (*The brigands set fire to the old house.*)
   contain an intransitive verb (*Swiftly the great building burned.*)
   or it may be a very short sentence fragment that stands alone. (*How sad.*)

2 A full stop is used at the end of a command sentence, a sentence that orders, compels or requires, a sentence which uses the imperative form of the verb.
   EXAMPLE: *Keep off the grass. Please sit down.*
   Have another cake.

3 Until recently full stops have been used after abbreviations such as *John Brown & Co. Ltd., Dr. D. Livingstone, Capt. Anderson of Hants., B.B.C., U.S.A.*
   Modern usage, no doubt hastened by the computer, has led to the exclusion of these marks (*John Brown & Co Ltd, Dr D Livingstone, Capt Anderson of Hants, BBC, USA*).
   It is therefore up to the individual to choose, but please, whatever you decide, be consistent. Do not use the abbreviation mark for some words and not for others.

4 It is worth remembering that mathematical and currency units such as *m, mm, cm, l, p, ins, km, cl, g, £* are usually written without the abbreviation full stop.

QUESTION MARK

1 The question mark (?) takes the place of a full stop at the end of a sentence which asks a question, which uses the **Interrogative** form of the verb.
EXAMPLE: *Are you coming with us? Is this the right book?*
Am I seeing things?

2 Note that the three questions above all require answers of sorts. There are some questions, however, where it may not be so obvious that an answer is required. **Rhetorical questions** (where no answer is normally required) must still be punctuated with question marks.
EXAMPLE: *What else can you expect? Who cares? Who knows?*

3 There are also questions such as *Isn't it a beautiful morning?* and *She looks lovely, doesn't she?* that may sound more like statements, but their grammatical structure is such that they are in fact questions and therefore they require the final question mark.

EXCLAMATION MARK

1 The exclamation mark (!) takes the place of the full stop at the end of a sentence which exclaims something. It indicates to the reader that what is being said is perhaps shouted or has a degree of urgency or requires stressing in some other way.
EXAMPLE: *Get out of here this instant! Never speak to me again!*
How rude you are!

2 It can also be used to indicate that perhaps a sentence is being said with sarcasm or humour, or is not to be taken too seriously as in:
I only hope I can be as fortunate!
She arrived in an elderly Rolls Royce and a large purple hat!

3 Exclamation marks are used after interjections such as *Oh! Sh! Ouch!*

4 It is used when calling to someone: *Tommy! Don't do that!*

5 Finally, a warning!
Exclamation marks can become addictive and whereas you may write to a friend and say   *He sent me two dozen red roses!!!!!!!!!!!!*
Roger, that is!!!! Of all people!!!!!!!!!
do keep the multiple use of the exclamation mark well away from formal writing and examination officers!

COMMA

Because there are so many uses of the comma it is easy for students to use them indiscriminately, littering their writing with commas like falling leaves in autumn. Do not do it! Only use a comma if you have a very good reason to do so, like the sixteen listed here.

1 Use commas in lists instead of *and* or *or*.
EXAMPLE: *Maggie went shopping and bought a red coat and a purple scarf and a pair of shoes and a belt.*
This would be better written as:
Maggie went shopping and bought a red coat, a purple scarf, a pair of shoes and a belt. Note that the final *and* is left in.
He was offered A or B or C or D. This becomes
He was offered A, B, C or D. Note that the final *or* is left in.

2 Use them in a list of adjectives or adverbs in the same way as in **1**.
EXAMPLE: *It was a huge, green, slimy, terrifying monster.*
(A list of adjectives.)
The swans glided past silently, gracefully and magically.
(A list of adverbs.)

3 Use commas to separate main clauses in a sentence.
EXAMPLE: *They arrived at the house, they burst in through the door, they took over our lives.*

4 Use commas to separate question phrases at the end of questions.
EXAMPLE: *You have read it, haven't you? I did lock the door, didn't I?*
These are sometimes called **Question Tags**.

5 To separate people's names when they are being addressed in a sentence.
EXAMPLE: *Jack, is this the house you built?*
A little spider, Mary, won't hurt you.
The correct term to address the second person is the **Vocative**.

6 To separate interjections when used as part of a sentence rather than standing alone.
EXAMPLE: *Oh, don't be so silly. Well, that is the end of that.*

7 To separate the words *yes, no, please, thank you* in sentences.
EXAMPLE: *No, he did not agree to play.*
Please, may I have some more?

8 To separate adverbs such as *meanwhile, however, nevertheless.*
EXAMPLE *The girls, meanwhile, were climbing the mountain.*
Nevertheless, the band continued to play.

Take care with the word *however*, which may be used in another way, not requiring separation by comma.
EXAMPLE: *However difficult it becomes, we shall not give up.*

9 To separate relative and subordinate clauses from the main clauses of a sentence.
EXAMPLE: *The concert, which is an annual event, was a great success.*
The man, who was quite elderly, leapt out of the window.
The view was wonderful, nothing but mountains and great skies.

10 A comma is needed to make the meaning quite clear when the word order of a sentence is inverted.
EXAMPLE: *We were happy walking until it started to rain.*
Inverted this becomes:
Until it started to rain, we were happy walking.

11 When writing direct speech, commas are needed in the following ways:
She said, "The rain will not last very long."
"Your room is dreadfully untidy," Audrey remarked.
"I have written," she complained, "but I doubt they will reply."

12 To separate towns, counties and countries.
EXAMPLE: *I will be flying from Bristol, England to Paris, France.*

13 In letter writing commas are used in various ways:

i to separate the parts of an address like:
33, East Street,
Ilminster,
Somerset, TA19 0AN.
ii A comma is placed after *Dear Mr Talbot, Dear Sir,*
iii A comma is placed after *Yours sincerely, Yours faithfully,*

However, today it is acceptable to leave out all the punctuation shown above when using a word processor, but do not do half-and-half: either include all punctuation or leave it all out.

14 Use commas to separate the component parts of dates and numbers.
EXAMPLE: *Today's date is Wednesday, 6th October, 1999.*
14,560,500.

15 Commas can be very useful to avoid ambiguity, as you can see in these sentences where the position of the comma can entirely change the meaning:

> *I am going to Birmingham perhaps, with John.*
> *I am going to Birmingham, perhaps with John.*

> *Opposite the house was a derelict building.*
> *Opposite, the house was a derelict building.*

Test Yourself 9 (q.3) p.57

APOSTROPHE

The apostrophe is becoming a neglected punctuation mark, perhaps because many people are not entirely sure how to use it and so they think they will play safe and leave it out. This is not a good idea and will not endear you to your examiner who may be extremely fond of this little flying comma.

It really is not difficult because the apostrophe has only two functions.

1 Use the apostrophe to show omissions – missing letters in contractions:
EXAMPLE: *I am – I'm, you have – you've. he is – he's, it is – it's,*
we will – we'll, they had – they'd, do not – don't.

There is little to go wrong there although people make mistakes and place the apostrophe in the wrong spot, especially when dealing with a negative. They write *do'nt, did'nt, wo'nt* instead of *don't, didn't, won't.*

2 The apostrophe is often used in dates to omit the century.
EXAMPLE: *The '39 – '45 War. The Class of '89.*

3 The apostrophe is used to show possession.
i *'s* is used to show ownership by a single person, place or object.
EXAMPLE: *Sebastian's coat, the dog's lead, the chair's leg,*
Bournmouth's seafront.

ii *s'* is used to show ownership by more that one person, place or object.
EXAMPLE: *The boys' showers, elephants' tusks,*
the different countries' flags.

iii *'s* and *s'* are also used with some units of measure to show possession.
EXAMPLE: *A week's holiday, two weeks' holiday,*
twenty-five years' service.

Note that possessive pronouns ending in *-s* (with the exception of *one's*) do not need apostrophes. It is a common error to write *her's*, *your's* and especially *it's* (see **1** on page 26) .

Test Yourself 9 (q.2) p.57

QUOTATION MARKS

Quotation marks may be double (" ") or single (' ').

1 Sometimes called **Speech marks**, they are used to enclose direct speech – the reporting of the exact words spoken by someone.
Although most printed novels in Britain today use pairs of single raised commas for this purpose, it is more acceptable in handwritten work to use doubles.

Here are several sentences to show the patterns of use of quotation marks:

a *She said, "The train will not be very long."*
b *"Your room is dreadfully untidy," Audrey remarked.*
c *"Come here, please," Mr Evans snarled. "I am not at all pleased."*
d *"Where are my socks?" shouted Harry.*
e *"Stop it!" he ordered. "Stop it immediately!"*
f *"We bought the radio in June," they wrote, "and it's never worked."*

You should notice that ...
in every case the first letter of the quotation is a capital.
in sentence:

> **a** there is a comma before the quotation starts.
> **b** a comma replaces the full stop at the end of the quotation.
> **d** *shouted* starts with a small *s*.
> **e** *he* starts with a small *h*.
> **f** the quotation is interrupted, *and* continues with a small *a*.

When you write dialogue remember that every time the speaker changes you must create a new line. (New speaker = new paragraph.)

2 Single inverted commas as speech marks are useful when a quote occurs within a quote.
EXAMPLE: *"I said, 'Don't do that!' didn't I?" Mary pleaded.*

3 Use quotation marks as described above when quoting someone's thoughts if the verb *to think* means *to say to oneself.*
EXAMPLE: *She thought, "Now what is going on here?"*

4 Use quotation marks in much the same way to enclose quotations from novels, plays, poems, famous speeches, and so on.

If the quotation is short it can be absorbed into the sentence.
EXAMPLE: *We arrived in Dorset in that "season of mists and mellow fruitfulness" when the countryside was at its most lovely.*

If, however, the quotation is longer it is clearer to set it out thus:
Rupert Brooke , the poet who died in 1915, wrote those famous words:
 "If I should die, think only this of me:
 That there's some corner of a foreign field
 That is for ever England."

Test Yourself 10 and 11 pp.58/59

INVERTED COMMAS

The punctuation marks (' ').
The terms **Inverted Commas** and **Quotation Marks** are becoming interchangeable but in fact they have separate uses.
Whereas Quotation Marks (also called Speech Marks) may be double or single, Inverted Commas are a pair of single raised commas with two main uses:

1 Use inverted commas to enclose the titles of books, plays, poems, radio or television programmes, newspapers and magazines.
EXAMPLE: *'The Mill on the Floss' by George Eliot,*
 'What Every Woman Knows' by J.M.Barrie,
 'The Darkling Thrush' by Thomas Hardy.
Note that the authors' names do not need to be placed within inverted commas.
 'Gardeners' Question Time' and 'Home and Away',
 'The Daily Mail' and 'Teen Scene'.

2 The second use of inverted commas is to enclose a word or words which need to be emphasised or stressed or highlighted for some other purpose.
EXAMPLE: *It was clear that he was a 'chip off the old block'.*
 The word 'led' is often misspelt 'lead'.
 Look out! Here comes 'Lord' Smith.
 She went to Paris in search of 'la vie Boheme'.

Test Yourself 11 p.59

COLON

The punctuation mark (:) is used within a sentence to explain or amplify what has come before it.

1 It may be used to indicate to the reader that there is something to follow such as a list, a quotation or an explanation/amplification.

EXAMPLE: A list. *The train will only stop three times: Birmingham, York and Edinburgh.*

A quotation: *Aladdin remembered the magic words: "Open Sesame!"*

Amplification: *They found the trunk: the gold was theirs for the taking.*

2 A colon may also be used in certain numbers.

EXAMPLE: *The reading was taken from Leviticus 18: 1 - 15.*
Today's date is 05: 08: 99. The time is 10:15a.m.
They outnumbered the enemy 4 : 1.

SEMI-COLON

The punctuation mark (;) is used to link two groups of very closely related words which could usually stand alone as sentences in their own right. Instead of using a full stop, the semi-colon is used to show a continuation of thought.

The two sentences may be related in three ways:

1 The second sentence is the cause of the first.

EXAMPLE: *He slipped on the pavement; the surface was extremely slippery.*

2 The second sentence is the result of the first.

EXAMPLE: *Pip tore down the shutters; light streamed into the dusty room.*

3 The second sentence gives more information about the first.

EXAMPLE: *We visited Edinburgh; it is such a beautiful city.*

It would have been possible to join the first example using *because*, the second with *and*, while the third might have used *which*, but using semi-colons will add variety to your writing.

Brackets

There are four kinds of brackets ( ), [ ], < >, { }. The first are called round brackets, the second are square brackets, the third are angle brackets and the fourth are called brace brackets. They are all always used in pairs.
For the purposes here we need only deal with round brackets.

1 Round brackets (in American English called parentheses) are used to enclose extra information added to the sentence, but without which the sentence would still make complete sense.
EXAMPLE: *Robin handed his gift (a large cabbage) to the Vicar.*

This could have been written using commas:
Robin handed his gift, a large cabbage, to the Vicar.

What, then, is the difference? Very little, but information in brackets is generally thought to be less important than information enclosed with commas.

Examples of correctly used brackets may illustrate the point.
William Shakespeare (1564 – 1616) is our most famous playwright.
I enclose my cheque for £14.00 (fourteen pounds).
They were a party to the North Atlantic Treaty Organisation (NATO).

There are a few points worth noting about the use of brackets:

a If a bracket closes at the same point as another punctuation mark, that mark should go outside the bracket, not inside.
EXAMPLE: *Sean (14), Sally (15) and Ravi (12) were the first to arrive (at 2.24).*

b The first word inside brackets should normally start with a small letter unless it is the beginning of a complete sentence within the brackets, or something like NATO (above).

Use brackets sparingly.
Too many of them, like the dash, can lead to a disjointed style of writing.

DASH

In formal writing it is much better to use brackets or commas to enclose information additional to the main part of the sentence.

However, the dash can be a useful punctuation mark if used sparingly and for a very specific purpose.

1 The dash can give an impression of informality so if that is your intention, use it.

EXAMPLE: *Hi there everyone! It's me – your hostess with the mostest!*

2 Dashes can also convey a sense of urgency.

EXAMPLE: *I'll be waiting for you – don't be late – don't forget your passport – at the station.*

3 Dashes are also useful when writing direct speech to show uncertainty or hesitancy.

EXAMPLE: *"I won't – er – that is – I'll try not to," she spluttered.*

HYPHEN

This punctuation mark (-) is shorter than a dash and it has four main functions:

1 The hyphen is used to separate the parts of some compound words.

EXAMPLE: *home-made, bird-bath, honky-tonk, full-bodied, post-war.*

It may well be asked why other compound words such as bedroom, godfather, bricklayer do not employ hyphens. Even dictionaries disagree but generally it would seem that at some time these words were hyphenated but over long usage they have dropped the hyphen.

2 The hyphen is used to join together words in a phrase.

EXAMPLE: *Jack-in-the-box, fly-by-night, a once-in-a-lifetime trip, through-and-through.*

3 A further use of the hyphen is to divide longer words at the end of a line. There are certain rules governing their use here:

a Split the word at a syllable like *screw-driver, hope-fully, dis-gusting* rather than *screwd-river, hopef-ully, disgu-sting* which are quite difficult to read when split between lines.

b Never split a word of one syllable.

4 The hyphen is also used in writing numbers as words.
EXAMPLE: *twenty-one and three-quarters.*

Whole numbers up to *ninety-nine* are hyphenated but beyond that they are not (*four hundred, five thousand* and so on)

ELLIPSIS

The omission of a word or words in a sentence is called **Ellipsis** – plural Ellipses (and occasionally **Eclipsis** – Eclipses) and is indicated by the punctuation mark of the same name (...) – three dots.
It may be used in several ways:

1 When leaving words out of a quotation so that just the important part remains.
EXAMPLE: *"Swear not by the moon ... that monthly changes ... lest that thy love prove likewise variable."*

2 At the end of a sentence it may be useful to tail off, either to indicate that it is becoming inaudible
EXAMPLE: *Into the distance they melted, their voices fading, fading ...*

or perhaps to leave the rest to the reader's imagination:
EXAMPLE: *He gazed into her eyes, took her hand, and then ...*

3 It is sometimes used to withhold an offensive word.
EXAMPLE: *"You... !" he snarled.*

Test Yourself 12 (Full Punctuation) p.60

Spelling

There are a number of basic **Rules of Spelling** that are useful to know but the English Language is such that there are always exceptions to the rules, waiting to catch out the unwary writer. Undoubtedly the way to good spelling lies in becoming interested in words and how they are formed; interest leads to awareness and finally to familiarity.

The *Spelling* section of this guide is divided into three parts: Rules, Lists of the most frequently misspelt words and, finally, a list of commonly confused words.

RULES

Four rules for changing singular nouns to plural

1 The simple way to change **singular** (one) into **plural** (more than one) is to add -*s*.
Example: *cat* becomes *cats, bell* becomes *bells, stone* becomes *stones.*

But ... there are exceptions:
If a noun ends in -*s*, -*sh*, -*ch*, -*x*, then add -*es*.
EXAMPLE *bus* becomes *buses, flash* becomes *flashes, church* becomes *churches, fox* becomes *foxes.*

2 If a word ends in -*y* with a consonant before it, change the -*y* to -*ies* to make it plural.
If a word ends in -*y* with a vowel before it, add -*s* to make it plural.
EXAMPLE: *baby* becomes *babies,*
city becomes *cities,*
boy becomes *boys,*
guy becomes *guys.*

3 For words ending in -*f* or -*fe* sometimes we just add -*s*.
But ... sometimes we change the -*f* to -*v*.
(You may need to use your dictionary.)
For words ending in -*ff* just add -*s*.

4 For words ending in a vowel plus -*o* we usually add -*s*; other words ending in -*o*, add -*es*.

SUFFIXES AND THE DOUBLING RULE

This rule applies when a suffix is added to words with one syllable, one short vowel and one final consonant.

If the suffix begins with a vowel, double the final consonant; if the suffix begins with a consonant, don't!

EXAMPLE: *shop + ing = shopping*
(suffix begins with a vowel so last consonant is doubled.)
sad + ness = sadness
(suffix begins with a consonant so final consonant is not doubled.)

SUFFIXES AND THE *SILENT e* RULE

This rule applies to words ending with a *silent e* such as *fate, hope, love.*

If the suffix begins with a vowel, drop the *silent -e*; if it begins with a consonant, don't! For this purpose -*y* counts as a vowel as well as *a,e,i,o,u.*

EXAMPLE: *fate + ful = fateful; love + ly = lovely;*
hike + ing = hiking; shine + y = shiny.

The rule does not apply to words ending -*ee*, so do not drop the final -*e*.

EXAMPLE: *flee + ing = fleeing, agree + able = agreeable.*

Words ending in -*ce* or -*ge* keep the silent -*e* before suffixes beginning with *a*- or *o*-

EXAMPLE: *courage + ous = courageous; trace + able = traceable.*

Words ending in -*ce* change the *e* to *i* before *ous*.

EXAMPLE: *space + ous = spacious; malice + ous = malicious.*

i BEFORE *e* EXCEPT AFTER *c*

This rule only applies to words which make an "*ee*" sound.

EXAMPLE: *chief, retrieve, believe, perceive, conceit, received*
but *weight, eighty, height, skein.*

There are exceptions like *seize, protein* and names like *Neil, Sheila, Keith.*

Words containing *ie* as two syllables do not follow this rule.

Example: *society, aliens, science, audience.*

NEGATIVE PREFIXES: *un-, dis-, mis-, in-, il-, im-, ir-.*

There is frequently confusion about which negative prefix should be added to which words. Here are a few rules which may help.

1 *un-* is the most common prefix and is almost always used with an adjective.
EXAMPLE: *happy – unhappy, kind – unkind, healthy – unhealthy.*

There are also a few verbs which take the prefix *un-* to form the opposite.
EXAMPLE: *do – undo, dress - undress, hinge – unhinge.*

2 *dis-* is mostly used with nouns and verbs.
EXAMPLE: *able – disable (disability); appear – disappear (disappearance).*

3 *mis-* does the same job as *dis-* but tends to mean *"badly"*.
EXAMPLE: *misprint – to print badly or incorrectly;*

4 *in-* is a frequent alternative to *un-* but there are several rules to learn about *in-*:
in- becomes *im-* when used in front of *b*, *m* or *p*
EXAMPLE: *imbalance, immature, impractical.*

in- becomes *il* when used in front of *l*.
EXAMPLE: *illogical, illiterate, illegitimate.* (Note the double *l*.)

in- becomes *ir-* when used in front of *r*.
EXAMPLE: *irregular, irrational.* (Note the double *r*.)

SUFFIXES: *-able, -ible.*

Some nouns and verbs can be turned into adjectives by adding *-able* or *-ible*. Unfortunately there are no rules about which to use and therefore you must use your dictionary to find which ending fits and then learn it.

It may help to know that *-able* is more common than *-ible*.

ENDINGS: *-er, -or, -ar, our.*

These endings all make more or less the same sound (*-er*) at the ends of words.
There are rules but they are full of exceptions, so you will need to learn many of the spellings.

1 *er-* is the most common ending.
It is always used to mean 'more something'.
EXAMPLE: *long – longer, high – higher, bright – brighter.*
(The comparative of adjectives)

Words ending in *-y* change the *y* to *i* before adding *-er*.
EXAMPLE: *shiny – shinier, sunny – sunnier, friendly – friendlier.*

Words ending in *d* or *t* follow the doubling rule (see above)
EXAMPLE: *sad – sadder, fit – fitter, hot – hotter.*

2 *er-* is also common as the ending for verbs,
EXAMPLE: *wander, deliver, suffer, scatter, bother, discover.*

3 Many people and their occupations end in *-er.*
EXAMPLE: *messenger, brewer, miner, teacher, waiter ...*
But ...

4 *or-* This ending usually follows *ct, at, it, ess, rr.*
EXAMPLE: *director, dictator, visitor, possessor, mirror.*

5 *ar-* This ending frequently follows the letter *l.*
EXAMPLE: *regular, collar, circular, similar, scholar.*

6 *our-* This ending is often found on abstract nouns.
EXAMPLE: *honour, humour, favour, endeavour, valour.*

ENDINGS: *-el, -le* OR *-al*

In the same way as there were no very clear rules about *-able* and *-ible* endings, there is little to help us decide about the *-el, -le* or *-al* endings to words.

apple, chapel, dental, fable, cancel, mortal, kettle, shovel, plural.

It's down to *Look and Learn* and eventually they will become familiar.

Spelling Part 2: Frequently Misspelt Words.

In a recent survey of GCSE students' work the following 100 words were found to be the most commonly misspelt.

accommodation	adolescence	advantageous	advertisement
aeroplane	aisle	antique	attachment
bachelor	benefited	calendar	campaign
ceiling	chemistry	christian	circuit
colleague	committee	computer	conscience
correspondence	criticism	deceitful	defendant
definitely	development	dictionary	disappear
discotheque	echoes	efficiency	embarrass
exaggerate	extraordinary	February	fictitious
foreign	forty	freight	gauge
ghastly	government	grammar	handkerchiefs
honourable	humorous	hygiene	illegible
innocence	instalment	irrelevant	irresistible
jeopardise	judgement	kilometre	knowledge
laboratory	liaison	lightning	literature
manoeuvre	massacre	medicine	Mediterranean
miniature	mischievous	moustache	murderer
narrator	necessary	neighbour	noticeable
occurrence	outrageous	parallel	parliament
particularly	picturesque	pigeon	plague
poisonous	pronunciation	questionnaire	receive
refrigerator	religious	restaurant	rheumatism
science	scissors	separate	sincerely
syllable	technique	tomatoes	unanimous
unnecessary	vicious	vocabulary	Wednesday

Spelling – Part 3: Frequently confused words

For various reasons the following pairs of words sometimes cause problems.

As a simple reference they are listed here together with simple definitions.

If you are ever in doubt about any of them, try writing a pair of simple sentences to demonstrate that you really do understand the differences.

accept:	receive
except:	leave out
advice:	(noun) opinion / information
advise:	(verb) recommend / inform
angel:	heavenly being
angle:	space between two lines that meet
ante-:	(prefix) before
anti-:	(prefix) against
assistance:	help
assistants:	helpers
astronomy:	study of stars and planets
astrology:	study of stars, planets & their supposed influence
beach:	sea-shore
beech:	tree
bored:	drilled/tired
board:	plank
breath:	(noun) air from lungs
breathe:	(verb) to draw air into lungs
bridal:	(adj.) of a bride or wedding
bridle:	(noun) horse's head harness
cellar:	underground room
seller:	someone who sells
check:	examine/slow down
cheque:	written order to Bank

cloths:	pieces of material
clothes:	garments
coarse:	rough
course:	direction/layer/series of lessons
compliment:	words of praise
complement:	to make complete
correspondence:	letters
correspondents:	writers of letters
councillor:	member of a council
counsellor:	adviser
current:	of present time/direction of flow
currant:	berry/dried seedless grape
dependent:	(adj) relying on
dependant:	(noun) someone who depends
desert:	barren waste land
dessert:	pudding or sweet course
device:	(noun) invention
devise:	(verb) plan/invent
discreet:	safe/cautious
discrete:	separate/autonomous
dying:	ceasing to live
dyeing:	colouring
eminent:	famous/distinguished
imminent:	about to happen
gaol:	prison
goal:	football target
gorilla:	ape-like creature
guerrilla:	commando-type soldier
hanger:	frame to hang clothes on
hangar:	building to house aeroplanes

led:	past tense of verb: to lead
lead:	heavy metal
licence:	(noun) a permit
license:	(verb) to authorise
lie/lie/lay:	three easily confused verbs:
lie – lying – lay – lain:	to rest/stretch out in prone position
lie – lying – lied:	to tell untruths
lay – laying – laid:	as in table or egg!
lightning:	electrical flashes of light
lightening:	making lighter
loose:	(adj.) insecure
lose:	(verb) mislay/not win
metre:	measurement of length
meter:	measuring instrument
miner:	one who works in a mine
minor:	lesser/one not of full age
past:	time gone by
passed:	past tense of verb: to pass
patience:	calm endurance
patients:	persons receiving medical treatment
personal:	one's own/private
personnel:	body of employed persons
practice:	(noun) custom/repeated exercise
practise:	(verb) to do repeatedly
principal:	chief/head of a college
principle:	rule/code of conduct
programme:	plan/list of event
program:	coded instructions to a computer
prophecy:	(noun) future prediction
prophesy:	(verb) to predict the future

quite:	adverb of degree to an extent
quiet:	with little or no sound
review:	critical study/assessment
revue:	musical entertainment
serial:	episode in a serial
cereal:	grain crop used as food
sew:	to stitch
sow:	to scatter seed
stationary:	still
stationery:	writing materials
suit:	matching jacket & trousers/skirt
suite:	set of rooms/furniture

Figures of Speech and Literacy Devices

Alliteration

This is a device rather than a figure of speech and it is frequently used in poetry. It is where a consonant is repeated, often at the beginnings of words.

EXAMPLE: *"Water, water, everywhere, and not a drop to drink."*
(Note *w-w-w* and *dr-dr*) *"Peter Piper picked a peck of pickled pepper." "And weeds in wheels grow long and lovely and lush."*

Analogy

A figure of speech is very much like a simile, in that two things are compared. In an analogy there will be clear similarities in certain features or qualities of the two things being compared.

EXAMPLE: *Time and tide wait for no man.*
Here *time and tide* are being compared and their ongoing, unstoppable qualities are evident.

There is another meaning to the word **analogy** to do with the formation and derivation of words, but that need not concern us here.

Anticlimax

In this kind of figure of speech there is a sudden change from dramatic, lofty or sublime sentiments to the feeble, trivial or ridiculous.
It is frequently used for comic effect.

EXAMPLE: *Well, you could have knocked me down with a sledgehammer.*
Clearly you expect the final word to be *feather* and the introduction of *sledgehammer* is unexpected and, as a result, humorous.

"When I'm good, I'm very, very good. But when I'm bad, I'm better." (Mae West)

Antithesis

Unlike **analogy** (above) where the things being compared bear similarities to each other, in antithesis there is a clear contrast or opposition of ideas, but in successful antithesis there will be a balance of words and ideas that serve to make the figure of speech memorable.

EXAMPLE: *"My words fly up, my thoughts remain below."* ('Hamlet)
"More haste, less speed."
"Light gains make heavy purses."

Assonance

This is something like alliteration but instead of consonants, the vowel sounds are repeated.

EXAMPLE: *"Down and around and the sound drowned out."*
"How now, brown cow?"

Of course there will always be assonance in rhyme: *flight – bright – white – knight. "The few who truly knew ... the cat that sat upon the mat."*

Bathos

This is similar to **Anticlimax** (above) but whereas in anticlimax the effect is deliberate, in bathos it is unintentional and something that has set out to be serious ends up being ridiculous. Take care when writing verse that you do not sacrifice too much for the sake of a good rhyme, resulting in bathos.

EXAMPLE: *"Beautiful Moon, with thy silvery light,*
Thou cheerest the Esquimau in the night;
For thou lettest him see to harpoon the fish
And with them he makes a dainty dish."

(William McGonagall.)

Cliché

A **cliché** is a phrase or expression which may once have been original and very effective but has become so over-used that it is now regarded as a stereotype, hackneyed or even trite.

EXAMPLE: *I think you are making a mountain out of a molehill.*
He made the supreme sacrifice. (Meaning that he died, usually in battle.)
At this moment in time I am speaking to you from the bottom of my heart.

Test Yourself 14 p.62

Colloquialism

A colloquialism is a word or a phrase – a figurative expression – that is used mostly in everyday speech, especially in conversation. Sometimes it is used in informal writing but it is perhaps safer not to use such expressions in a formal essay or speech because the line between a colloquialism and slang is a very fine one.

EXAMPLE: *I needed someone to give me a hand but he led me up the garden path and unfortunately I came a cropper. It really gets up my nose to see Charlie being given such a hard time.*

Test Yourself 14 p.62

Dyads – also called Doubles

These are simply pairs of words which almost always go together.

EXAMPLE: repetition of the word

neck and neck	*better and better*

alliterative pairs

time and tide	*bright and breezy*

opposite pairs

this and that	*up and down*

repetition of meaning

hale and hearty	*rough and tumble*

rhyming pairs

fair and square	*high and dry*

Test Yourself 14 p.62

Euphemism

A Euphemism is when a word or phrase is substituted for one which might be thought to be unpleasant or distasteful. For example, instead of saying that someone has died, some say that they have *passed away*; sometimes people refer to the lavatory as *the facilities* or any number of other names.

Test Yourself 15 p.63

Hyperbole (pronounced *high-per-bow-lee*) is overstatement or exaggeration for the sake of effect. It is not intended to deceive anyone and sometimes it is used humorously.

EXAMPLE: *Please accept ten thousand apologies.*
I shall move Heaven and Earth to get it for you.
We went to the play and we almost died of boredom.

In advertising the term to *hype*, meaning to build up a product through overstating or exaggerating its properties, comes from the word *hyperbole*)

Test Yourself 15 p.63

Irony is a figure of speech in which one thing is said but the opposite is implied.

EXAMPLE: *Well that will do a lot of good, I must say.*
(It will be clear from the way in which the words are said that whatever it is will do no good at all.)

Dramatic irony occurs in a play when the audience becomes aware of a situation while it remains unknown to the characters, so that the audience may foresee the (often tragic) outcome in such a way that the characters' words and actions take on a greater significance.

Litotes

(pronounced *lie-tote-ease*), is the opposite of **hyperbole** – it is understatement, often achieved by using a negative to convey the opposite meaning.

EXAMPLE: *He's not exactly my best friend.*

(meaning: *He is my enemy.*)

She is not a bad player.

(meaning: *She is quite a good player.*)

Test Yourself 15 p.63

Metaphors

Like a **simile**, a **metaphor** is a figure of speech used to convey an image, but whereas a simile says that something is like or as something else, a metaphor takes it one step further and the thing we are talking about actually takes on the qualities of something else.

EXAMPLE: *The lava slithered down the mountain **like** a snake.*

(**simile** – lava *like* a snake)

A huge golden snake of lava slithered down the mountain.

(**metaphor** – the lava *is* a snake)

In a metaphor one thing is assumed to be another for comparison?

It is easy to get carried away (metaphor?) when you start using lots of metaphors and one danger to look out for is the **mixed metaphor**.

EXAMPLE: *Time waits for no man and Joe was about to embark on the journey of life.*

Jane tried to pour oil on troubled waters when she saw the fire in Harry's eyes.

Draw a veil over it, bury the past and let sleeping dogs lie.

On the other hand, mixed metaphors, used deliberately, can be amusing.

EXAMPLE: *"That's the way with these directors, they're always biting the hand that lays the golden egg."*   (Sam Goldwyn)

Test Yourself 13 p.61

Metonym

A word or an expression which is used in place of another, with which it has a close connection..

EXAMPLE: People may talk about *The Turf* when refering to horse-racing.

The Crown may be used when talking about the Monarchy.

The bottle = alcoholic drink. *The Bar* = the legal profession.

Test Yourself 14 p.62

Onomatopoeia

(pronounced *on-oh-mat-oh-pee-yah*)

This refers to words whose sound suggest their meaning.

    EXAMPLE: *Ducks quack, the sword clanged, the hiss of a snake,*
                 leaves rustled, the buzzing of bees, the fire crackled,
                 the horse's hooves clattered.

Oxymoron

This can be a very effective device, using a combination of words which appear to be contradictory. It is frequently used for humorous effect.

    EXAMPLE: *The silence was deafening. It was a bittersweet comedy.*

Personification

We have looked at similes and metaphors as figures of speech, used to create images in our reader's or listener's mind.

If we carry the metaphor a little further so that an object without life (like a train or a tree) is given human or animal qualities, this is called **personification**.

    EXAMPLE: *"The train roared into the station, a great fire-eating dragon,*
                 breathing smoke from its nostrils, its eyes glowing."
                 Of course a train doesn't roar and it does not have nostrils or
                 eyes, but by comparing it with a dragon in this way we can
                 create a very clear picture.
                 "The lonely tree shivered and moaned in the icy wind and
                 longed for the spring when once again leaves would clothe its
                 bent and battered body."
                 For effect the writer has given the tree all sorts of human
                 feelings that, of course, it would not really have.

The simplest kind of personification is created by giving a humanising adjective to a non-human noun.

    EXAMPLE: *a spiteful bramble, a friendly shore, a threatening sky.*

Here is a list of such adjectives: *inviting, sleeping, lonely, welcoming, proud, angry, selfish, disapproving, growling, grateful, impatient, humble, laughing, happy, hungry, forgiving, cheeky, well-dressed, hopeful, suffering.*

Another kind of personification is to use humanising verbs and adverbs with non-human nouns.

    EXAMPLE: *The wind howled angrily down the chimney.*
                 The brook chuckled happily over the stones.

Test Yourself 13 p.61

Proverb

A **proverb** is a short, well-known saying which often contains a great deal of wisdom.

EXAMPLE: *A fool and his money are soon parted.*
Once bitten, twice shy.
Too many cooks spoil the broth.
A cat has nine lives.
The truth is stranger than fiction.
Fair exchange is no robbery
Proof of the pudding is in the eating.
Pride goes before a fall.
Necessity is the mother of invention
Many hands make light work

Test Yourself 16 p.64

Pun

A pun is a figure of speech made up of a word or a sentence with two meanings. They are often quite amusing but may raise groans.

EXAMPLE: *The wind blew down the chimney.*
He made his victims eat cornflakes until they exploded – he was known as a cereal killer.
Card in newsagent's window: *Young woman wants cleaning.*

Simile

We use words to convey meaning.

To explain more fully what we mean, we may compare one thing with something else, to make the image clearer.

EXAMPLE: *Eric ran away from them quickly.* Makes sense but does not create much of a picture in the reader's mind.
Eric ran away from them like a fox being chased by a pack of hungry hounds. This compares Eric with a fox and the picture that the reader receives is far more effective.

Look at these examples from three famous writers:
"'Oh Bertie,' she said in a low voice like beer trickling out of a jug." "He paused and swallowed convulsively, like a Pekingese swallowing a pill." (Two from P.G.Wodehouse)

"... making it momentary as a sound, swift as a shadow, short as any dream, brief as the lightning in the collied night."
From Shakespeare to show how short something is.

"Bats... hanging upside down like rows of disgusting old rags."
(D. H. Lawrence.)

These **figures of speech** are called **similes** and you may have noticed that in the examples above they are all introduced by the words *like* or *as*.

Test Yourself 13 p.61

Tautology

This is the term used to refer to the unnecessary repetition of the same thing in different words.

EXAMPLE: *They arrived in succession, one after the other.*
He died from a fatal injury.
She was an unmarried spinster.

Zeugma (a.k.a. Syllepsis)

A figure of speech in which a word (frequently a verb) is followed by two words which would not normally be found together. The element of unexpectedness is often amusing.

EXAMPLE: *Alice arrived in a large hat and a flood of tears.*
"Mr Pickwick took his hat and his leave." (Dickens)

Test Yourself 18 (Questions – Figures of Speech) p.67

1 This passage contains 40 nouns.
Sort them into two lists: 24 **common nouns** and 16 **proper nouns**.

'The Tempest' is a romantic drama by William Shakespeare. It tells the
story of Prospero, Duke of Milan, and his daughter, Miranda, who live on a
strange, enchanted island where they are served by Ariel, a spirit, and
Caliban, a misshapen monster. Prospero, who has learned magic arts,
summons up a tempest and causes a ship to be wrecked on the shores
of the island. The vessel was carrying the King of Naples and his son,
Ferdinand, together with other members of the court, including his own
villainous brother, Antonio. The play is full of magic and there is some
excellent comedy provided by Stephano, a drunken butler, and Trinculo,
the court jester. This was Shakespeare's last completed play, written in
1611, and one of his most frequently performed today.

2 What is the **collective noun** for each of these groups?
locusts, lions, dancers, sailors, horses, governors, fish, swallows, cubs,
magistrates

3 Sort these nouns by gender: **masculine, feminine, common, neuter**.
actress, bachelor, boar, bridegroom, Briton, bull, choir, coffee, computer,
duckling, fiancee, fire-eater, heiress, hostess, housewife, kingdom,
peacock, scissors, soldier, traffic, tree, usher, vicar, widow.

4 Turn these 20 **adjectives** into **abstract nouns**.
good, true, happy, poor, stupid, dangerous, religious, jealous, pitiful,
merciful, miserable, lenient, successful, gracious, sad, innocent, anxious,
heroic, courageous, able.

5 Turn these 20 **singular nouns** into **plurals**.
berry, wolf, mother-in-law, thief, echo, church, hobby, shelf, louse, hero,
passer-by, cactus, dwarf, city, tomato, roof, bus, solo, larva, stimulus.

1   Agreement. In these sentences change all **singulars** to **plurals**.

     a   I watched the bird building its nest in the tree.

     b   The child was given a large amount of money for its birthday.

     c   The fiddler on the roof could be a wolf in sheep's clothing.

     d   When she died I was left my aunt's house.

     e   He was having difficulty with the Maths test.

     f   There was a mouse in the old lady's room.

     g   My neighbour has bought a cottage in Cornwall.

     h   This tap's washer is worn and that is why it is dripping.

2   In this passage change the tense from **present continuous** to **past simple.**

> I am writing this sitting on a beach in Greece. I am the only person here and it is incredibly peaceful. The sun is shining, the waves are gently lapping the shore and from the twisted olive trees behind me there is the continuous singing of the cicadas. Even as I am looking, a small herd of goats are making their way past me and heading for the sea. Now they are drinking the salt water and it looks as if they are eating the pebbles. How peculiar! A yacht has sailed into the bay and the goats are bleating loudly and running away.

3   In these sentences change the verbs from **active voice** to **passive**.

     a   He kicked the ball through the open window and it smashed a vase.

     b   They would open the doors at nine and start the auction at ten.

     c   The Jewish people proclaimed the State of Israel in May 1948.

     d   In 1967 Britain announced a ban on meat from countries with foot-and-mouth disease.

     e   Judi Dench plays 'M' in the latest 007 films.

     f   In London they have constructed the largest ferris wheel in the world.

     g   A seven-year-old girl won the recent Chess Championship.

     h   Writers often use the passive voice of the verb to sound less direct.

1 Identify the verbs in these sentences, including auxiliary verbs and state what tense and what kind of verb each one is.

   a After the earthquake the tower collapsed.
   b Leave that and follow me.
   c Were you following me?
   d My dream is to live on a desert island.
   e We had been walking for two hours.
   f By Tuesday she will have painted the whole house.

2 Complete this table of irregular verbs.

Present	Past	Past Participle	Present	Past	Past Participle
give	gave	given	drink		
saw			seek		
know			speak		
freeze			fight		
spring			ring		
cut			throw		
write			hurt		
swim			weave		
shake			tread		
rise			ride		

3 Instead of using the phrasal verbs in each sentence think of a single verb that means the same.

   a Romulus and Remus were *brought up* by wolves.
   b It is difficult to *make out* what she has written.
   c I'll *ring* you *up* this evening.
   d The storm *set back* their plans but they finally *set off* today.
   e Please *hold on* while I *look into* the matter.
   f After all she had *been through* still she would not *give up*.
   g The deal *fell through* when the manager *passed away*.
   h If the weather *clears up* we may well *go in for* the competition.

1 Pick out and list the 22 **descriptive adjectives** contained in this short passage by Herman Melville.

> "It was a clear steel-blue day. The firmaments of air and sea were hardly separable in that all-pervading azure; only, the pensive air was transparently pure and soft, with a woman's look, and the robust and man-like sea heaved with long, strong, lingering swells. Hither and thither glided the snow-white wings of small, unspeckled birds; these were the gentle thoughts of the feminine air; but in the deeps, far down in the bottomless blue, rushed mighty leviathans, sword-fish, and sharks; and these were the strong, troubled, murderous thinkings of the masculine sea.

2 Using the 'O S A C O M P' rule, insert the adjectives into each sentence.

    a She was wearing a ...., ..., ... shirt. (*silk, old, lovely*)
    b We bought a ...., ..., ..., ... house. (*Victorian, big, town, brick*)
    c The car was ...., ... and .... . (*small, blue, new*)
    d This was her ...., ..., ..., ... dress. (*long, velvet, favourite, green*)
    e We bought a bunch of ...., ..., ... grapes. (*Spanish, green, sweet*)
    f It was a ...., ..., ..., ..., ... stick. (*oak, heavy, walking, nasty, black*)

3 Form adjectives from these nouns:
      hero, gold, contempt, pride, miracle,
      France, north, table, school, beast.

4 Form adjectives from these verbs:
      choose, suggest, deceive, speak, enchant,
      lose, defend, vary, irritate, exclude.

5 In each sentence, replace the adjectival phrases with single adjectives:

    a The owner *of the factory* buys steel *from Wales* and *from Germany*.
    b As well as her job *in a school* Jane worked as a dancer *in a disco*.
    c We had a holiday *in the country* as well as one *at the seaside*.

6 List the **possessive adjectives**, the **demonstrative adjectives** and the **interrogative adjectives**.

1 In these sentences pick out the **adverbs** and **adverbial phrases** and make three lists of **manner** (*how*), **time** (*when*) or **place** (*where*).

  a Eventually we arrived at the restaurant before lunchtime.
  b The current flowed swiftly and relentlessly down the river.
  c Soon the roar was frighteningly louder as we were tossed carelessly over the rapids and around the rocks.
  d Without hesitation she walked out of the room and for several minutes there was silence,
  e In the early morning the swans landed on the lake, beautifully and gracefully.
  f Before sunset Sir Gawain was mortally wounded beneath his arm.

2 In these sentences the adverbs are in italic print.
What type is each adverb?
You must choose from **interrogative** or **relative adverbs**, **adverbs of degree**, **frequency** or **probability**.

  a *How* will we find it if it is *too* dark?
  b That was *definitely where* I left it.
  c *Most days* the bus is *very* late but *perhaps* it will be early today.
  d *Maybe* we will *never* learn *when* it happened but *why*?
  e *Yes*, we can *certainly* see *where* the tide *usually* reaches.
  f *Why* they left was *undoubtedly very* strange but *possibly* it was the rain.
  g *No*, I *never completely* understood *why* he was *only ever* asked *once*.

3 Answer these questions about adverbs.

  a What kind of **adverbial phrase** is *three times a week*?
  b What kind of **adverbial phrase** is *for a few days*?
  c What kind of **adverbial phrase** is *behind the shed*?
  d What kind of **adverbial phrase** is *in a friendly tone*?
  e *more suitably, later, more slowly* are each what kind of adverb?
  f *fastest, most clearly, most likely* are examples of what kind of adverb?
  g When there are, adverbs of time, place and manner within the same sentence, what is the accepted order?

1 Complete this table of pronouns - subject form, object form, possessive pronouns and reflexive pronouns.

	1(s)	2(s)	3(s)	3(s)	3(s)	1(pl)	2(pl)	3(pl)
Subject								
Object								
Possessive								
Reflexive								

2 Copy each sentence and put a **subject** or **object pronoun** into the gaps.

a He wrote to .... (3s) but she did not reply to .... (3s).
b They are all faster than .... (1s) but .... (1s) am stronger than .... (3pl).
c She is taller than .... (3s) but .... (3s) is heavier than .... (3s).
d You gave it to .... (3pl) and .... (3pl) sold it to .... (1pl).
e ....(1s) saw it was ....(3pl) and ....(1s) knew ....(3pl) had come for ....(1s)
f The card was from ....(1s) but ....(2s) thought ....(3s) was from ....(3s).

3 Insert **I** or **me** into these sentences, changing the order if needed.

a .... and Sylvia are looking for a flat.
b The cat was rescued by Ann and .... .
c You and .... have been invited to the Simmons' party.
d Harry, ... and Brett have been selected to play.
e .... and my neighbours are going to Scarborough.
f The parcel was addressed to .... and my sister.

4 For these sentences choose the correct personal pronouns.

a The contest is between ...... and .... (*them/ they* ... *us/we*)
b It's Goodnight from ...... and .... (*he/him* ... *I/me*)
c You and ...... will play ...... and his brother. (*I/me* ... *he/him*)
d ...... and our two friends are going to stay with ...... and their parents. (*us/we* ... *them/they*)
e ...... , ... and my aunt are going out for the day. (*she/her* ... *me/I*)
f ...... and their crowd have been unpleasant to ...... and my friends. (*they/them* ... *I/me*)

1 Insert **interrogative pronouns** into these sentences.

    a .... would you like to do this evening?
    b .... is your favourite author?
    c .... is your favourite food?
    d .... is your favourite restaurant?
    e Of these two books .... do you prefer?
    f This is my coat but .... is this?
    g .... is paying for the tickets?
    h To .... shall I send this card?

2 Use relative pronouns to join these pairs of sentences.

    a This is Ann. She lives at 7 Muchelney House.
    b That is the castle. It was lived in by the Mary, Queen of Scots.
    c Ralph is a consultant. His work takes him all over the North East.
    d The trees are growing. They will form a windbreak.
    e You are the owner. I wrote to you last week.
    f Eva is a great cook. We are eating with her on Sunday.

3 Correct the errors of agreement in these sentences.

    a One can only be expected to do his or her best.
    b None of the pictures were properly framed.
    c No-one among the campers are allowed out after ten o'clock.
    d Each of the twelve teams have to play two matches.
    e Few of the boys had taken his own tin-opener.
    f If any one of you have been abroad, put up your hand.

4 Rewrite these sentences so that they do not include sexist language.

    a If a driver has an accident he must report it at once.
    b The nurse on duty must sign the report form herself.
    c If a pupil gains less than 20% he will have to re-sit the test.
    d A volunteer must offer his services himself or he cannot be accepted.
    e When a patient sees his name on the board he must report to the desk.
    f Each resident is responsible for clearing away his own rubbish.
    g He who hesitates is lost!
    h Every man for himself!

1 Join these sentences with conjunctions without using the same one twice.

    a The film had ended. She was really sad.
    b Jack could go swimming. Jack could stay at home.
    c It rained a lot. We still enjoyed ourselves.
    d The caller was not Lucy. The caller was not Aaron.
    e I had eaten oysters. I felt quite ill.
    f Lily ran down the road. Lily missed the bus.

2 What is the difference between a **coordinating conjunction** and a **subordinating conjunction**?

3 Insert the most suitable prepositions into these sentences.

    a He was angry .... (*at/with*) us.
    b I refuse to comment .... (*on/about*) the reports.
    c Divide the the cake .... (*between/among*) the six of you.
    d They say that black is the opposite (*to/from/of*) white.
    e This book was different (*to/from/than*) any other that I had read.
    f Stop beating .... the bush and clutching .... straws and lay .... the law.

4 Insert these eighteen preposition into the passage below:
round, to, towards, beside, behind, by, into, against, through, inside, across, after, opposite, down, from, among, at, along.

> I crouched .... the wall .... the Bank, my back pressed .... the hard stone. Late shoppers hurried .... the street, glancing ....window displays, while I searched .... them for Jake. Suddenly he came.... the corner, ran .... the street and .... the hill .... me. He came .... a blue door and was .... it and .... the building. I raced .... him and .... the doorway I looked.... a crowded bar. Jake was .... the counter.... someone I never expected to see again.

5 Are the words in italic conjunctions, prepositions or adverbs?

    a He arrived *before* the party and did not leave *until* two a.m.
    b Someone had been *through* this door *since* teatime *when* we closed it.
    c I have kept this *for* him *since* he left *but* now our friendship is *over*.
    d She arrived *before* him *and* waited *outside* *until* she saw his car.
    e I went *through* *until* I came *across* the code *but* have not seen it *since*.

1 Rewrite this passage in nine complete sentences.

> McRae approached the door there was something quite forbidding about its appearance in the distance a bell could be heard when he pulled the iron handle then footsteps echoed along what sounded like a stone passageway as the door slowly creaked open McRae could hear his own heart beating like a cornered animal he did not know whether to stand his ground or run around the side of the partly opened door a head appeared the strangest pair of eyes peered into his at that instant he felt himself being taken into the control of something quite alien.

2 Apostrophes: rewrite each sentence, inserting the apostrophes that have been missed out.

   a Its nine oclock and shes sure shell be late.
   b Were wondering why we cant see whats stopping its wheels going.
   c Maries hoping shes been chosen for the part but it isnt likely.
   d Mikes teacher collected the childrens toys for the schools bazaar.
   e Mr Jones team had to wait outside the boys changing room.
   f James uncle painted all the houses front doors apart from ours.
   g Dannys dogs hurt its paw which is why its whining.
   h I dont know what time theyre arriving but theyll probably be late.

3 Commas: Rewrite these sentences with all the necessary commas. In each case say why commas are needed.

   a I went out to buy nails screws glue paint wallpaper and brushes.
   b He wore a dreadful old baggy green Aran wool sailing pullover.
   c He said "I'm afraid I've broken your pen."
   d You will come wont you?
   e Following in Dad's footsteps Joe who is nine wants to be a vet.
   f We are hoping meanwhile to do some shopping.
   g I will be flying from Madrid Spain to Paris France.
   h Today is Friday 31st December 1999.

1 Rewrite these sentences in **reported speech**.

   a John said, "I am going to be late for the meeting."
   b "I think someone has been in here," whispered Mary.
   c "Does Mr Smithers live here?" the policeman asked.
   d "We are going to Dublin next week," Deirdre announced.
   e "Open wide," the dentist ordered me, "so that I can have a look."
   f "Now go to the office," Mrs Harris explained to me, "and say that I sent you."

2 Here is a report of a speech. Write out that speech in the exact words in which it would have been spoken - i.e. as **direct speech**.

At a recent meeting in Little Highton, Mrs Mounce told members of the Leisure Committee - her fellow villagers - that she was delighted that so many of them had gathered there that evening, especially when the weather was so dreadful, and so she thanked them for making the effort. She hoped that they would think it worthwhile when she told them the good news. Mrs Mounce reported that she had received a letter that morning from the Chair of the County Council and she said that she knew the Committee would be thrilled to know that he had promised to give them his full support. She went on to tell the meeting that a cheque for £2000 had been received from an anonymous donor, which meant that there was enough money in the fund for them to begin the first phase of the building work. Mrs Mounce then said that she would hand them over to Mr Jolliff who had offered to oversee the site clearance.

3 Rewrite this extract from a play as **reported speech**.

Jack: I am extremely pleased to meet you, Mrs Yard.
Ann: Please call me Ann. I don't think of you as a stranger.
Jack: Harry spoke of you often. You meant a great deal to him.
Ann: As he did to me, I assure you, Jack. Will you tell me about it?
Jack: Of course. It's why I came, but now that I'm here, it's not easy.
Ann: Please, I beg of you, just tell it as it happened. I won't interrupt.
Jack: Well ... er ... that is ... there were only six of us left. Harry was my second-in-command. I ordered him to take two of the others and go south. The other three of of us went north.

1 Punctuate the following sentences containing direct speech.
As well as quotation marks, do not forget the correct placement of
commas.

   a Ann said I have never known such cold weather for August.
   b That really is a ghastly colour Jasper remarked.
   c The leaves are dangerous he warned take care that you do not slip.
   d Has anyone seen my shorts shouted an embarrassed Arthur.
   e Stop it Jack ordered now stop it at once.
   f I bought this watch in June she complained and it's never worked.
   g This is my pen. Do you doubt it? I should think not! he snapped.
   h Paul said he was going to Kent, adding do you want to come?

2 Punctuate these sentences which contain quotations and titles as well as
direct speech.

   a julie said on saturday nights I like to watch blind date and have a
really hot curry
   b has anyone found marks copy of the homework series miss owen asked
   c and elizabeth mr davis announced will play lady capulet in romeo and
juliet
   d humbug cries scrooge in a christmas carol by dickens
   e have you not read the silver chair katie asked youll love it
   f who said a horse a horse my kingdom for a horse the questionmaster
asked

3 Rewrite this passage in paragraphs, inserting all necessary punctuation.

what are you looking for ellen asked a book hugh snapped graciously a
book what book if you must know its great expectations he said i need
it for school tomorrow where did you have it last she enquired if i knew
that id know where it was now hugh shouted all right theres no need to
be rude ellen countered if you like you can borrow my copy you did say
great expectations didnt you yes thanks very much grinned hugh.

1 Set out this letter, using full punctuation.

> 27 hinchcliffe gardens over hillverton somerset ta49 9gt tel 01569
> 248594 19th april 00 greystoke travel 12 coronation avenue
> bridgwater dear sirs i saw your recent advertisement for a trainee
> travel assistant in the county gazette i am aged fifteen and am about
> to take my gcse exams and it has always been my ambition to work in
> the travel industry although i will not be available until the middle of
> june i would be really pleased if you would consider me for the position i
> try to look smart and i am reliable and trustworthy as you will see
> from the enclosed reference from my form teacher my predicted
> grades may not be the highest but i think i can promise to make up for
> them in hard work i hope to hear from you yours faithfully john marks

2 Rewrite this passage from Hugh Walpole's 'Judith Paris' from which all
punctuation has been omitted. It should be in six paragraphs.

> the old man rolled his head nay nay im past everything but
> dreaming damn my bones dont you worry my pretty when
> youve had a pain in your leg a long while its a kind of friend
> then he added quite casually as though he were saying
> nothing at all georges may be riding over from whitehaven
> today her heart began to hammer georges paris aye hes
> grown a fine young man but hell burn his fingers one of these
> days hes in with a lot o rogues ive told him but he dont listen
> thinks he can manage them very confident young man is
> georges before she could say anything or even reason with
> herself about her foolish excitement emma furze joined them
> judith saw that she had smartened herself she had a black
> hoop and a silver band in her dark hair she looked really
> handsome as she stood there there was something both
> foolish and good in her face her black eyes were large and
> brimming with emotion at the slightest excuse her breast
> would heave and swell she looked at judith with a childlike
> smile of pleasure i saw a fine man on a horse and said to
> myself he's come to take her away i was tortured by the
> anxiety my dear you need be tortured no longer no fine
> gentleman shall take me away

1 Complete these somewhat hackneyed similes.

As fit as a ....   As cool as a ....   As dull as ....

As poor as a ....   As sick as a ....   As flat as a ....

As free as ....   As thick as ....   As sober as a ....

As tough as ....   She swims like a ....   He ate like a ....

2 In these, list all the examples of similes, metaphors and personification.

  a Time marches on and waits for no man.

  b Suddenly the car's engine spluttered, coughed and died.

  c The sea was on fire, a sheet of gold, as the sun submerged itself beneath the waves.

  d Whole regiments of tombstones marched across the French hillsides.

  e They surged through the doors like a hungry plague of locusts.

  f The old house was waiting to welcome back its children.

  g The massive cliffs stood proud and defiant, defending our country against the angry sea.

3 In these lines from 'A Tale of Two Cities' Charles Dickens used some vivid imagery. What devices has he used to create his desired effects.

> "The mildewy inside of the coach with its damp and dirty straw, its disagreeable smell, and its obscurity, was rather like a larger dog-kennel. Mr Lorry, the passenger, shaking himself out of it in chains of straw, a tangle of shaggy wrapper, flapping hat and muddy legs, was rather like a larger sort of dog."
>
> "From the dimly lighted passages of the court the last sediment of the human stew that had been boiling there all day was straining off."
>
> "There was a steaming mist in all the hollows, and it had roamed in its forlornness up the hill, like an evil spirit, seeking rest and finding none. A clammy and intensely cold mist, it made its slow way through the air in ripples that visibly followed and overspread one another, as the waves of an unwholesome sea might do."

Clichés

1 Rewrite these sentences in plain English, without the clichés.

   a A little bird told me that it was a matter of life and death.
   b He was a rough diamond but he had a heart of gold.
   c Don't call it a day - there's light at the end of the tunnel.
   d At the eleventh hour he decided to turn over a new leaf.
   e It's raining cats and dogs but the coast is clear.
   f At this point in time we should stand on our own feet.
   g As a nation we have played the game from time immemorial.
   h He was the apple of his mother's eye but to his father he was like a red rag to a bull.

Colloquialisms

1 Rewrite these sentences in plain English without the colloquialisms.

   a They gave me a hard time but I stuck it out and showed I had guts.
   b We're all under a cloud today because old Fred's kicked the bucket.
   c It was down to them so they'll have to face the music.
   d I was at a loose end so I took the bull by the horns and rang him.
   e This is a wind-up. You're having me on but I'm not taken in easily.
   f We tried to lead him up the garden path but he didn't fall for it.
   g He'd blotted his copybook by taking forty winks and was under a cloud.
   h Things are in a right mess so let's get cracking and play ball.

Dyads

1 Complete these word pairs:

They left him *high and* ....
He died for *Queen and* ....
He looked quite *hale and* ....
I am *ready and* .... for work.
The weather is *wet and* ....
Consider the *ins and* ....

She is *alive and* ....
It was *fair wear and* ....
It was *part and* .... of his complaint.
It was explored *through and* ....
Poor man is *down and* ....
Let's have more *give and* ....

Euphemisms

1 Each sentence contain euphemisms. Rewrite each in plain English.

a She ran a shop which specialised in dresses *for the fuller figure.*

b Are you a *senior citizen*?

c Not only am I *a little off-colour* but I am getting *hard of hearing.*

d Uncle Harry is *no longer with us*, having *given up the struggle* and *departed this life.*

e Her clothes *had seen better days* and it was clear that she was *financially embarrassed.*

f Following a *difference of opinion* with an *officer of the law* after *taking a drop too much*, he found himself a *guest of Her Majesty.*

g I think you are *being somewhat economical with the truth.*

h As they approach the *evening of their life* they are going to live in *a retirement hotel.*

2   Now make up a polite euphemism for the following:

a crippled person	a dustman	a person with spots
a stutter	thin	a tumbledown cottage
a very short person	a fat man	a nasty smell

Hyperbole / Litotes

3 Decide which of the following sentences contain examples of hyperbole and which litotes.

a He had the feeling that she was not exactly displeased to see him.

b I waited for ages and ages and almost died of boredom.

c When the firework exploded I must have jumped ten feet in the air.

d She was not averse to a drink and clearly had had more than a few.

e Mount Everest is not the easiest mountain in the world to climb.

f Her daughter was worth her weight in gold to her.

g Boa constrictors are not the easiest pets to look after.

h Having run like lightning she was boiling hot.

4 Now rewrite the sentences from Question **3** in plain English.

Metonym:

1 What is understood by these metonyms and metonymous expressions?

    a His first son, the baronet, *entered Parliament*, his second *was called to the Bar*, while the third son *went into the Church*.

    b *Whitehall* decided on £4.00 *per head*.

    c *Across the water* in France he swore allegiance *to the Crown*.

    d His bank account swiftly plunged from being *in the black* to being seriously *in the red*.

    e *The deep* claimed him.

    f He was hounded by *the press*.

    g *The pen* is mightier than *the sword*.

    h She had ambitions for *the Oval Office*.

Proverbs:

1 Complete the following proverbs. What does each one mean?

    a Don't cut off your nose to ....

    b Curiosity ....

    c What can't be cured must ....

    d You can lead a horse to water but ....

    e Fair exchange is ....

    f The end justifies ....

    g All things come to ....

    h He who sups with the Devil should have ....

    i March comes in like a lamb and goes out ....

    j There's many a slip twixt ....

    k .... shouldn't throw stones.

    l .... red sky in the morning, shepherd's warning.

    m .... is another man's poison.

    n .... gathers no moss.

    o .... is master of none.

    p .... is sauce for the gander.

    q .... never boils.

    r .... does not make a summer

    s .... is in the eye of the beholder.

Copy and complete these sentences:

1 *Who? Whom? Whose? Which? What?* are examples of .... pronouns.

2 The accepted order for adjectives is ...., ..., ..., ..., ..., ..., ..., ...

3 Commands such as *Stop! Wait! Listen!* are called .... verbs.

4 *Who, whom, whose, which* are examples of .... pronouns.

5 As well as being verbs in their own right, *to be, to do, to have* can also serve as .... verbs.

6 Words joining together units of equal status are called .... conjunctions.

7 *One, none, any, other* are examples of .... pronouns.

8 Adverbs answering the questions *How? When? Where?* are called adverbs of .... , ... and ....

9 When referring to a verb (*to write, to speak, to hope*) that form is known as the ... of the verb.

10 *deeper, happier, more difficult* are examples of .... adjectives.

11 He spoke in a friendly tone. The final four words of that sentence are an example of an .... of ....

12 A verb that does not have a direct object is called an .... verb.

13 There are two voices to a verb: .... and ....

14 *She will be travelling* is an example of the .... tense.

15 A word joining a dependent clause to the main clause of a sentence is called a .... conjunction.

16 Verbs made up of more than one word (usually verb + preposition) are called .... verbs.

17 *fastest, most clearly, most willingly* are examples of .... adverbs.

18 *Oh! Sh! Ouch! Help! Whew! Look out!* are known as ....

19 Words such as *herd, team, choir,* are called .... nouns.

20 In regular verbs the .... is formed by adding *-ed* to the infinitive.

21 Adverbs answering the question *How often?* are called adverbs of ....

22 *She had travelled* is an example of the .... tense.

Complete these sentences.

1 When a writer repeats consonants, often at the beginnings of words, as in *"The ragged rascal ran around the town"*, this is called .....

2 Repeated vowel sounds, as in *"around the town"* is called ....

3 *"It's no good crying over spilt milk after the horse has bolted"* is an example of a ....

4 A device that combines apparently contradictory words such as *"bittersweet"* or *"The silence was deafening"* is called ....

5 *"A stitch in time saves nine"* is an example of a ....

6 A device using deliberate understatement, as in *He is not the world's greatest actor* is called ....

7 The opposite of Question **6**, using exaggeration, as in *" I thanked her a thousand times"* is called ....

8 .... is the name give to words that actually sound like what they mean, words like *hiss, clank, splash, hoot.*

9 .... is the term used to refer unnecessary repetition as in *"He was a bachelor and he was not married."*

10 A phrase or expression that may once have been original but has become so overused as to become a stereotype is called a ....

11 A simile can often be easily recognised by the words .... or ....

12 Pairs of words which almost always go together, such as *bright and breezy, rough and tumble, time and tide* are called ....

13 When we give an inanimate object human or animal qualities, sounds or feelings, this is called ....

14 A figure of speech in which one thing is said but the opposite is implied is called ....

15 Figurative expressions that are used in everyday conversations, and border on being slang, are called ....

16 When we substitute a word or phrase for something that might be considered unpleasant or distasteful, this is called a ....

17 A .... is a figure of speech where one thing takes on the qualities of another for the purpose of comparison.

On this page there are a number of errors of various kinds.
See how many you can find and then rewrite the page correctly.
(I found 110!)

1 It has been said "if you become a teacher, by your'e pupils you'l be
tuaght.

2 Me and my friend Vikram are hopeing to become referrees and if we
practice hard enough we should get our licenses in febuary. Mr Lang
selected Vikram and myself out of twenty-seven boys which applied,
less than in previous years. Vikrams father died when he was seven. Hes
got one brother, called Maan, but Vikrams the oldest. On saturday he
often comes round for breakfast and mum always say, "Bacon and eggs
are a good way to set us up for the day". We haves a laugh but we dont
say nothing because mums real generous. She always give us a bag of
cakes to share between all of us in our team.

3 There were seven men but none of them have come forward.

4 'Please can I have a copy of "Lord of the Flies" by "William Golding"
'the lady asked the bookseller.

5 Jack was lieing when he said he was laying in bed when the goose layed
the golden egg.

6 The goverment advised all young persons aged between forteen to
twenty to definately register, dependant on the areas they lived in.

7 Homophones:
This storey takes plaice in the passed, in daze of your, and is the tail of
too buoys, won the sun of a barren wile the other's farther was a night.
One mourning at the our of ate the pear road of too fined an old manner
house on the boarders of Whales in witch they had herd a mien, bade
nave lived.   A long lain lead them to clime over a warn style, threw a
gait, across a mote to a grate read door on witch they wrapped with
there soared. Nought butt piece and quite did they here and then they
new there journey had bean in vane.

Copy the grid then fill in the crossword

Clues Across

1 Hackneyed expression.
4 Group of words
7 Repeated vowel sounds
9 Current fashion
10 Husband of countess
11 Half a horse?
12 Address to audience
14 Pattern of sound
16 Unintended anticlimax
18 Fights
20 Sick
21 Molten rock
23 Kind of lily
24 Substituted word
25 As lines for signing
26 Greek nymph

Clues Down

1 Punctuation marks
2 Upper or lower for letters.
3 Sufficient
4 Actor
5 Care to hurry (anag.)
6 Visual symbol
7 Descriptive word
8 Underground compound noun
13 Onomatopoeic pidgin English?
15 Feminine possessive pronoun
16 Song or poem
17 Homophone on the side
18 Held responsible
19 Something like a figure of speech
22 Relative noun
23 Abbreviation, now if not sooner.

Glossary

Glossary of Terms used in the Study of English

Abbreviation: A shortened form of a word or phrase.
It may take various forms.
i the initial letters of words such as *B.B.C.* (British Broadcasting Corporation), *PC* (Personal Computer).
ii the shortened form of a word as in *ad* (advertisement), *flu* (influenza).
iii shortened forms such as *Dr.* (Doctor), *Sgt.* (Sergeant) *etc.* (et cetera).

Abstract noun: The name given to something which has no material existence.
EXAMPLE: *beauty, excitement, anxiety, success. Nouns which have material existence are called Concrete Nouns.*   *Study p.6*

Acronym: A word formed from the initial letters of other words.
EXAMPLE: *NATO*   (North Atlantic Treaty Organisation),
AIDS   (Acquired Immuno-Deficiency Syndrome)

Active voice: The form of the verb used when the subject performs the action.
EXAMPLE: *"We found mushrooms in the grass."* (The Passive Voice would be *"Mushrooms were found in the grass."*)   *Study p.9*

Adjective: A word added to a noun to describe or modify that noun.
EXAMPLE: *elderly, green, happy, Irish, old.*   *Study p.12*

Adjective of Quantity: A word used with a noun to show quantity.
EXAMPLE: *fifty, many, most, seventh, less.*   *Study p.12*

Adverb; A word that modifies or qualifies a verb, adjective or another of the eight kinds of adverb. (See under.)   *Study p.14*

Adverb of manner: This is the most common kind of adverb and it tells us *how* something happens. Most adverbs of manner end in *-ly* and are formed from adjectives.
EXAMPLE: *happy – happily; beautiful – beautifully; slow – slowly.* *Study p.14*

Adverb of time: This tells us *when* something happens.
EXAMPLE: *tomorrow, soon, later, already.*   *Study p.14*

Adverb of place: This tells us *where* something happens.
EXAMPLE: *here, there, somewhere, nowhere.*   *Study p. 14*

Adverb of degree: This tells us *how much* something happens.
  EXAMPLE: *too, very, rather, only.*   *Study p.15*

Adverb of Number or Frequency: This tells us *how often* something happens.
  EXAMPLE: *once, sometimes, never, usually.*   *Study p.15*

Adverb of Probability: This tells us *how sure* we are about something.
  EXAMPLE: *yes, no, perhaps, probably.*   *Study p.15*

(Interrogative) Adverb: This is used for asking questions.
  EXAMPLE: *How? Where? When? Why?*   *Study p.15*

(Relative) Adverb: These include the same words as **Interrogative Adverbs**
(above) but they are used in sentences which are not asking questions.
  EXAMPLE: *He did not know **how** he would find it.*
         *She could not think **where** she had lost it.*   *Study p.15*

Agreement: A verb should agree with its subject in person and number.
  EXAMPLE: *They is coming to tea.*
         (This is wrong because *They* (the subject) is plural, whereas *is*
         is singular.) Of course it should read:
         They are coming to tea.   *Study p.8*

Allegory: This is a form of story which has two meanings – the second with
a deeper and more significant meaning and with characters who represent
vices or virtues, with names like Sloth and Despair.
A famous example is '*The Pilgrim's Progress*' (John Bunyan 1678).

Alliteration: A device used frequently in poetry where a consonant, usually
initial, is repeated.
  EXAMPLE "*Water, water, everywhere, and not a drop to drink*"
         (*w-w-w-dr–dr*)   *Study p.42*

Anagram: A word made from the letters of another word.
  EXAMPLE: *cheater* is an anagram of *teacher*.

Analogy: This is a figure of speech, very like a simile, in which two things
are compared or equated.   *Study p.42*

Anticlimax: A figure of speech in which there is a sudden change from
dramatic, lofty or sublime sentiments to the feeble, trivial or ridiculous.
It is frequently used for comic effect.   *Study p.42*

Antithesis: A figure of speech in which ideas are contrasted or opposed. Although the words themselves may be opposed, they are usually well balanced.

    EXAMPLE: *"My words fly up, my thoughts remain below."*   *Study p.42*

Antonym: A word opposite in meaning to another word.

Apostrophe: The punctuation mark (') used for two purposes: to indicate the omission of letters in words such as *don't, I'll, he'd, we've*; to show possession as in the *cat's basket, the men's room.*   *Study p.26*

Article: A word used before a noun to show what it refers to. The Definite Article = *the*; the Indefinite Article = *a* or *an*, *some*.

Assonance: The repetition of vowel sounds.

    EXAMPLE: *"How now, brown cow?"*   *Study p.43*

Ballad: Originally this term referred to a simple song. It has developed to refer to a song or poem written in verse about an event (often tragic) and told impersonally in verses of four lines, frequently with a rhyming pattern of *a b c b*.

Bathos: This is very similar to **Anticlimax** (See above) but whereas in anticlimax the effect is deliberate, in Bathos it is frequently unintentional.

    Study p.43

Bibliography: A list of books or articles on a particular subject or by a particular author or a list of the sources used in the preparation of a book or essay.

Blank Verse: Verse that does not rhyme but is usually written in lines of ten syllables. (See below **Iambic Pentameter**.)

Brackets: Round brackets ( ) are punctuation marks used to separate supplementary or explanatory information which would otherwise interrupt the main flow of a sentence.

In American English they are called Parentheses.   *Study p.30*

Capital Letter: Its main uses in punctuation are as follows:
    i: to indicate the beginning of a sentence;
    ii: to indicate **Proper Nouns**. (See below)   *Study p.20*

Caricature: A portrayal of a person in which certain characteristics are exaggerated for comic effect.

Character: In literature any person portrayed in a play, novel or poem is referred to as a character.

Clause: A clause should contain its own subject and a verb.
It is more than a phrase, but less than a sentence.

Clerihew: A humorous poem of four lines with a rhyming pattern *A–A–B–B*.
It is about a person whose name forms the first line.
It is named after its inventor, Edmund Clerihew Bentley.
    EXAMPLE: *Sir Christopher Wren*
                  Said, "I am going to dine with some men.
                  If anyone calls
                  Say I am designing St. Paul's."

Cliché: A phrase or expression which has become so over-used that it has largely lost its effect and is generally regarded as stereotypical or hackneyed.   *Study p.43*

Climax: An intense or high point in a literary work, especially in drama.

Collective Noun: The name for a special group of people or animals.
    EXAMPLE: *choir* (of singers), *herd* (of cattle), *school* (of whales).
    Study p.6

Colloquialism: An informal word or phrase, a figurative expression, used in everyday speech, especially conversation. While not quite slang, this kind of expression is generally regarded as unsuitable for formal speech or writing.
    Study p.43

Colon: The punctuation mark (:) used within a sentence to explain or amplify what has come before it.   *Study p.29*

Command: More properly this is called the **imperative** form of a verb.
It gives an order.
    EXAMPLE: *Be quiet. Help me. Take the next turning.*   *Study p.10*

Comma: This punctuation mark (,) is used within the sentence to separate words, phrases and clauses.
It has many uses but is frequently over-used.
The comma may never be used to replace a full stop.   *Study p.24*

Common Noun: The name of a general (not specific) person, place or thing.
    EXAMPLE: *girl, village, knife.*   *Study p.6*

Comparative: This term refers to the form of adjectives and adverbs between **Positive** and **Superlative**. (see below).

> EXAMPLE: *big, bigger, biggest; bright, brighter, brightest; slowly, more slowly, most slowly; often, more often, most often.*

The comparative may be used to compare two objects whereas the superlative form is used to compare three or more.

Compound Word: A word made up of two or more other words or parts of words.

> EXAMPLE: *holiday-maker, battle field, doorstep, tin-opener, bedroom.*

It may well be asked why some of these compound nouns are hyphenated and others are not. Even dictionaries will disagree, but generally it seems to come down to usage where after long and established use the hyphen is dropped. (See **Hyphenation** below.) *Study p.31*

Conditional tense: This tense of a verb is formed by using the words *would* or *should* in order to refer to the future in the past. Almost invariably a sentence using this tense will use the word *if* to introduce the conditional.

> EXAMPLE: *The puppy was very small* (past) *and looked as if it would not live.* (future in the past).

Conjunction: A word or group of words that connects together other words or groups of words.
Common conjunctions include: *and, but, so, because, although, if, while, as soon as, as well as, yet.* *Study p.19*

Conjunctive: This is a word or a phrase that functions as a conjunction (see above).
Common conjunctives include: *however, meanwhile, at that time, therefore, otherwise, soon afterwards.*
Modern usage is leading to the words **conjunctive** and **conjunction** becoming interchangeable and therefore those words that are strictly speaking conjunctives are coming to be considered structural conjunctions.

Consonant: A speech sound or letter of the alphabet other than a vowel.

Contraction: A shortened form of a word or words by leaving out letters, frequently vowels.
I am becomes *I'm.* Also: *-'s* (is/has), *-n't* (not), *-'re* (are), *-'ve* (have), *-'d* (had/would). *Study p.26*

Coordinating Conjunction: A word used to join together units of equal status. Coordinating conjunctions include such words as *and, but, so, or, yet, either... or, neither... nor.* (See also **Subordinating Conjunctions** below)

Couplet: Two successive lines of verse, usually rhyming and of the same metre.

    EXAMPLE   *"Your hands than mine are quicker for a fray;*
               My legs are longer though, to run away."

Dead metaphor: A figurative expression that may have started life as a metaphor but has become absorbed into our language to the extent that it is is no longer considered a metaphor but is accepted as a literal expression.

    EXAMPLE: *the break of day, a chair leg, to foot the bill, to catch a cold, a bottleneck.*

Definite article: Simply the word *the* used to determine a specific noun.

Demonstrative pronoun: *This, that, these, those.*
It points out or demonstrates what it stands for and stands alone as the subject or object of the verb.

    EXAMPLE: ***That** is more expensive than **this**.*   *Study p.18*

Demonstrative adjective: These may be the same words as the Demonstrative Pronouns listed immediately above. The difference is that the adjective does not stand alone but is linked to a noun.

    EXAMPLE: ***this** computer, **that** book, **these** children, **those** houses.*
            The definite and indefinite articles (*the, a, an, some*) may also be considered to be demonstrative adjectives.   *Study p.12*

Descriptive adjective: An adjective of quality which usually answers the question *What kind of ...?*

    EXAMPLE: *happy, old, quiet, soft, fluffy, broken, bright, solid, straight.*

Dialogue: The words spoken by characters in a play or story.

Direct speech: Speech reported using the precise words spoken and as such usually included within quotation marks.

    EXAMPLE: *"I am going to Canterbury," said the traveller.*   *Study p.27*

Double negative: The use of two negative words in a single clause sentence in such a way that they cancel each other out.
Common errors made this way include: *I don't have none. I haven't done nothing.*

If in doubt as to why those sentences are incorrect, explore why these are the exact opposite: *I have none. I have done nothing.*

Doubles: see **Dyads** below

Dramatic irony: The irony that occurs in a play when the audience becomes aware of a situation while it remains unknown to the characters, so that the audience may foresee the (often tragic) outcome in such a way that the characters' words and actions take on a greater significance.   *Study p.44*

Duologue: A dialogue between two persons.

Dyads: Pairs of words which almost always go together.
   EXAMPLE: *rough and tumble, fair and square, bright and breezy.*
                                                                       Study p.44

Elegy: A sad or serious poem or song; sometimes a lament for the dead.

Ellipsis: A series of three dots (...) used to show that part of a sentence has been omitted.   *Study p.32*

Epigram: A short, witty saying.

Etymology: The study of words and their origins.

Euphemism: A word or phrase which is substituted for one which may be regarded as unpleasant, distasteful or embarrassing.
   EXAMPLE: Instead of saying that someone *has died*, we may say that he
        has passed away.   *Study p.44*

Exclamation mark: The punctuation mark (!) used after exclamations and strong commands. It is also usually found after an interjection.
   EXAMPLE: *Hey! Hush! Ouch!*   *Study p.23*

Farce: Comedy based on improbable happenings.

Feminine: In grammatical terms the gender of certain nouns such as *waitress, lioness, cow, queen, bride.*   *Study p.7*

Fiction: Works invented by the imagination such as stories and novels.

First person: See under **Person.**

Future tense: The form of the verb which is used for actions which will take place at some time in the future. Within that definition there are three subtle differences listed below: *Study p.10*

Future simple tense: This is formed by adding *will* or *shall* to the infinitive.

    EXAMPLE: *I will run, you will see, she will fly.*   *Study p.10*

Future continuous tense: This is formed by *will* or *shall* + *be* + the Present Participle (that part ending in *-ing*).

    EXAMPLE: *I will be running, you will be seeing.*   *Study p.10*

Future perfect tense: Here the action being described will have been completed at some time in the future. It is formed by *will* or *shall* + *have* + the past participle.

    EXAMPLE: *I will have run, you will have seen*   *Study p. 11*

Haiku: A form of poem which originated in Japan. It does not need to rhyme but it has a strict pattern of three lines of *5 – 7 – 5* syllables. The subject matter is frequently to do with Nature.
They can be very simple and hauntingly beautiful word pictures.

    EXAMPLE: *A flitting firefly! Look!*
               Look there! I start to call,
               But there is no-one. (Taigi)
The word itself comes from the Japanese *hai* (amusement) + *ku* (verse).
The plural is **haiku**, not haikus.

Homograph: A word that is spelt the same as another but has a different meaning and pronunciation.

    EXAMPLE: *sow* (plant seed) / *sow* (female pig)
               lead (cause to go) / *lead* (heavy metal).   *Study p.38*

Homonym: A word that is spelt and pronounced the same as another but has a totally separate meaning.

    EXAMPLE: *fair* (just) / *fair* (entertainment)
               soil (verb: to make dirty) / *soil* (earth).   *Study p.38*

Homophone: A word that is pronounced the same as another but has different spelling and meaning.

    EXAMPLE: *tea / tee, whacks / wax, side / sighed.*

Hyperbole: Overstatement or exaggeration used for the sake of effect.

    EXAMPLE: *"I've told you a thousand times to stop that."*   *Study p.44*

Hyphen: This punctuation mark (–) is shorter than a dash and it has three main functions.

i It is used to separate the parts of some compound words.
EXAMPLE: *home-made, bird-bath, honky-tonk, full-bodied, post-war.*

ii It is used to link together words in a phrase.
EXAMPLE: *Jack-in-the-box, fly-by-night, through-and-through.*

iii It is used between the syllables of a word when it is necessary to split that word between consecutive lines. The hyphen should come at the end of the first line, never at at the beginning of the second line. *Study p.31*

Hyphenation: When used with compound nouns the hyphen can be very useful sometimes to distinguish between meanings.
EXAMPLE: *re-cover* (as in a chair); *recover* (as from an illness).

Study p.31

Iambic pentameter: A line of verse consisting of ten syllables arranged in such a way that there are five stresses.
EXAMPLE: *When for-ty win-ters shall be-siege thy brow.*

Imperative form of verb: Verbs in this form all give an order.
EXAMPLE: *Be quiet. Help me. Take the next turning.*
(Also known as the **Command form** – see above.) *Study p.10*

Indefinite article: Simply the word *a, an* or *some* used to determine a noun.

Indefinite pronoun: It takes the place of any unspecified person, place or thing and can include words such as: *one, none, any, other, some, each, either, neither, everybody, somebody, much, more, most.* *Study p.18*

Indirect speech: See **Reported speech**

Infinitive of verb: The basic form of a verb from which most other parts of a verb are formed. It is always introduced by the word *to.*
EXAMPLE: *to run, to see, to fly, to hope, to eat, to think, to be.*

Study p.7

Innuendo: This is where something is insinuated, hinted at rather than openly stated.
It is often made in reference to a person and tends to be malicious.

Interjection: An exclamation or emotional noise.
EXAMPLE: *Oh! Sh! Ouch! Help! Whew! Look out!*

Notice that they are usually used with exclamation marks. *Study p.19*

Interrogative adverb: See under **Adverb**.

Interrogative pronoun: It stands in for a noun in sentences which ask questions: *Who? Whom? Whose? Which? What?*   *Study p.17*

Intransitive verb: A verb which does not take a direct object:
    EXAMPLE: *The snow fell. The winds blew. The children played.*
                (See also **Transitive verb** and compare.)   *Study p.7*

Inverted commas: The punctuation marks (' '). The terms *Inverted Commas*, and *Quotation Marks* are frequently becoming interchangeable but in fact they have quite separate uses. Whereas Quotation Marks (also called Speech Marks) may be double or single, Inverted Commas are a pair of raised single commas with two main uses.
i To enclose titles of books, plays, TV or radio programmes, films, etc.
ii To enclose a word or words which need to be emphasised or stressed, which may be slang or foreign.   *Study p.28*

Irony: A figure of speech in which one thing is said but the opposite is implied.
    EXAMPLE: *Well, that will do a lot of good, I must say.*
                Meaning that whatever it is will do no good at all.
                                              Study p.44

Jargon: Words or phrases developed for use within a particular group or subject and sometimes difficult for outsiders to understand.

Limerick: A humorous poem of five lines with a rhyming pattern of *A-A-B-B-A*. There are usually three stressed beats in the *A* lines and two stressed beats in the *B* lines.
    EXAMPLE   *There was an old man of Darjeeling*
                  Who got on a train bound for Ealing.
                  It said on the door,
                  "Please don't spit on the floor.
                  "So he got up and spat on the ceiling.
                (Edward Lear)

Litotes: Understatement, often achieved by using a negative to convey the opposite meaning.
    EXAMPLE: *She is not a bad player.* meaning: *She is quite a good player.*
                                              Study p.45

Lyric: A term used to to describe a particular kind of poetry in which the writer expresses personal thoughts and feelings.

Lyrics: The words of a popular song.

Malapropism: The unintentional misuse of a word by confusing it with another of a similar sound.
> EXAMPLE: *"She's as headstrong as an allegory on the banks of the Nile."*
> (*allegory* instead of *alligator*.)

(Named after Mrs Malaprop, a character in Sheridan's play, "The Rivals" written in 1775.)

Masculine: In grammatical terms the gender of certain nouns such as *nephew, hero, boy, stag, bull.*   *Study p.7*

Melodrama: A particular kind of play, full of suspense and tending to be rather over-dramatic and emotional. Very popular in the Nineteenth Century.

Metaphor: Like a simile, a metaphor is a figure of speech that conveys an image. While a simile says that something is *like* or *as* something else, a metaphor goes further and what is being talked about actually takes on the qualities of something else.   *Study p.45*

Metonym: A word or expression which is used in place of another, with which it has a close connection. For example, people talk about *the turf* to mean horse racing, *the Crown* to refer to the Monarchy or *the bottle* to mean alcoholic drink.   *Study p.45*

Metre: This is the term used in Poetry to describe the rhythmic arrangement of stressed and unstressed syllables in a line.

Mixed metaphor: The unsuitable combination of metaphors, often leading to slightly ridiculous images;
> EXAMPLE: *"Jane tried to pour oil on troubled waters when she saw the fire in Harry's eyes."*
> *Study p.45*

Monologue: A long speech made by one performer.

Non sequitur: Something which does not follow.
A statement which has little relevance to what preceded it.

Noun: The name of a person, place or thing. There are various kinds of Nouns – **Common, Proper, Collective, Abstract** (all described in this Glossary) plus **Singular, Plural, Masculine and Feminine**.   *Study p.6*

Object: That part of a sentence which receives or is affected by the action of the verb.

> EXAMPLE: In *Harry fed the cat. Harry* is the subject, the verb is *fed*, and the object (that which receives the action) is *the cat*.   *Study p.7*

Ode: A poem which is often addressed to a person or celebrates an event and which, as a general rule, contains noble sentiments.

Omission marks: A single apostrophe may be used to indicate missing letters. (See **Contraction**). Three dots may be used to indicate missing words. (See **Ellipsis**)

Onomatopoeia: Words which suggest their meaning by the sound they make.

> EXAMPLE: *hiss, quack, sizzle, crackle.*   *Study p.46*

Oxymoron: The combination of words which appear to be contradictory:

> EXAMPLE: *the silence was deafening.*   *Study p.46*

Palindrome: A number, word or phrase that reads the same from right to left as left to right.

> EXAMPLE: *1991. Madam I'm Adam, Live not on evil.*

Paragraph: A section of a piece of writing devoted to one idea, separated by a change of thought, person, time or place.
It is defined by starting a new line.

Parenthesis: A word, clause or sentence inserted as a kind of afterthought between brackets or dashes into a sentence which would be grammatically correct without it.   *Study p.30*

Parentheses: ( ) The American term for a pair of brackets (usually round).

Parody: A humorous, sometimes satirical imitation of a person or literary work or of a particular style.

Passive voice: The form of the verb where the subject is the receiver of the action.

> EXAMPLE: "*Mushrooms **were found** in the grass.*" The Active Voice would be "***We found** mushrooms in the grass.*"   *Study p.9*

Past tense: The form of the verb which is used when the action has already occurred. Within this definition there are three subtle differences listed below.   *Study p.10*

Past simple tense: Here it is understood that the action has taken place at a particular time in the past. In regular verbs the past tense is formed by adding *-ed* to the infinitive.
  EXAMPLE: *walk – walked, hope – hoped.*

With irregular verbs it is formed differently.
  EXAMPLE: *run – ran, see- saw, fly – flew.*

Past continuous tense: Here it is understood that the action was taking place over a period of time in the past.
It is formed by adding *was* or *were* to the **Present participle**.

  EXAMPLE: *I was running, you were seeing, she was flying, we were*
          hoping, you were eating, they were thinking.   *Study p.10*

Past perfect tense: (Also known as the **Pluperfect tense**)
Here it is understood that the action has taken place and been completed at a time earlier than some time in the past. It is formed by adding *had* to the past participle.
  EXAMPLE: *I had run, you had seen, he had flown, we had hoped, you had*
          eaten, they had thought.   *Study p.11*

Past participle: In regular verbs this is formed by adding *-ed* or *-en* to the infinitive.
  EXAMPLE: *seen, hoped, eaten.*
In irregular verbs it is formed in other ways.
  EXAMPLE: *flown, thought.*
It is the part of the verb used in perfect and passive tenses.   *Study p.8*

Pentameter: A line of verse having five main stresses, usually referred to as feet. (See **Iambic pentameter** above.)

Person: The First Person (*I, me, we, us*) denotes the person speaking or writing. The Second Person (*you*) denotes the person being spoken or written to. The Third Person (*he, him, she, her, it, they, them*) denotes the person being spoken or written of.   *Study p.8*

Personal pronoun: Used in place of a noun, the personal pronoun may take the subject or object form as follows:

Subject form: *I   you (s)   he   she   it   we   you (pl)   they.*

Object form: *me   you   him   her   it   us   you   them.*   *Study p.17*

Personification: When inanimate objects (like a tree or the wind) are given animal or human qualities for the sake of effect.

    EXAMPLE: *The lonely tree shivered in the cruel, biting wind.*

Study p.46

Phrase: A group of words which form a unit within a clause/sentence.

Pluperfect tense: See **Past perfect**.

Plural: A word form indicating more than one, rather than **Singular**, indicating just one.

Possessive adjective: These words tell you something about a noun like who the owner of that object is. The Possessive Adjectives are *my, your, his, her, its, our, their.*   *Study p.12*

Posessive pronoun: A word used without a noun to show ownership. *mine, yours, his, hers, its, ours, yours, theirs.*   *Study p.17*

Predicate: This is a term which is not used a great deal nowadays, but you may come across it and it is therefore as well to know what it means.
It simply refers to that part of a clause or sentence which makes a statement about the subject.

    EXAMPLE: *Harry* (subject) *fed the cat* (predicate).

Prefix: Letters added to the beginning of a word or word-root to modify its meaning.

    EXAMPLE: *unhappy, displeased, misplace, incorrect, illegal, international, maladjusted.*   *Study p.35*

Preposition: A word which indicates position, time or direction.

    EXAMPLE: *to, at, before, after, since, on, off, under, above.*

Composite prepositions consist of more than one word.

    EXAMPLE: *out of, in front of, next to.*   *Study p.19*

Present tense: The form of the verb which is used when the action is happening now. Within this definition there are three subtle differences. listed below: *Study p.10*

Present simple tense: Here it is understood that the action happens now, once.

    EXAMPLE: *I run, you see, he flies, we hope, you eat, they think.*

Study p.10

Present continuous tense: Here it is understood that the action is continuing to happen now.

    EXAMPLE: *I am running, you are seeing, he is flying, we are hoping,*
               you are eating, they are thinking. *Study p.10*

Present perfect tense: Here it is understood that the action has taken place at this time.

It is usually formed by adding *has* or *have* to the past participle. (See above.)

    EXAMPLE: *I have run, you have seen, he has flown, we have hoped,*
               you have eaten, they have thought. *Study p. 11*

Present participle: This is a part of a verb formed by adding *-ing* to the infinitive.

    EXAMPLE: *running, seeing, flying, hoping.* *Study p.8*

Pronoun: A word which takes the place of a noun. It can only be effectively used of course once the noun in question has already been referred to so that we know what is being talked of. There are seven types of pronoun: **Personal, Possessive, Reflexive, Interrogative, Demonstrative, Relative, Indefinite.** (See above & below). *Study p.17*

Proper nouns: The names of particular people, places and things.

    EXAMPLE: *Scotland, Shakespeare, Buckingham Palace.*
           They always start with capital letters. *Study p.6*

Propaganda: Material – written, spoken or visual – that is intended to persuade or convince others to adopt ideas or believe information.

Proverb: A short, well-known saying which often contains a great deal of wisdom.

    EXAMPLE: *Too many cooks spoil the broth.* *Study p.47*

Pun: A figure of speech made up of a word or a sentence with two meanings. It is often quite amusing.

    EXAMPLE: *The wind blew down the chimney.*
           He made his victims eat cornflakes until they exploded – he
           was known as a cereal killer. *Study p.47*

Question mark: The punctuation mark (?) used at the end of a sentence to indicate that it is a question. *Study p.23*

Quotation marks: The punctuation marks (" ") or (' '), used to enclose words or lines from a work of literature or words actually spoken by someone. (Also called **Speech marks** when used in this way.) Although most novels nowadays enclose speech in single inverted commas, the correct practice for most forms of writing is to use double. Should a quotation occur inside the double inverted commas, those words should be enclosed in singles to avoid confusion.

    EXAMPLE: *"I said, 'Don't do that!' didn't I?" Mary pleaded.*   *Study p.27*

Reflexive pronouns: Refers back to the subject of the sentence.
Pronouns: *I, you* (s), *he, she, it, we, you,* (pl) *they.*
Reflexive Pronouns: *myself, yourself, himself, herself, itself, ourselves, yourselves, themselves.*   *Study p.17*

Relative adverbs: See under **Adverb**.

Relative pronoun: *who, whom, which, whose, that.* A relative pronoun relates one part of a sentence to another by standing in for a noun already used and telling us more about it.

    EXAMPLE: *The trees are growing which will hide the view.*   *Study p.18*

Reported speech: Also known as **Indirect speech**, as opposed to **Direct speech**, it is a report of what was spoken without quoting the exact words. As such Reported Speech does not require Speech Marks or Quotation Marks.

    EXAMPLE: *Jane said, "I am hungry."* (Direct Speech) becomes *Jane said that she was hungry.* (Reported Speech.)   *Study p.27*

Review: A critical assessment of a book, play, poem, concert, film etc. Not to be confused with **Revue** (See below.)

Revue: A form of light entertainment consisting of songs, dances and sketches.

Rhetorical question: A question to which there is normally no answer required or expected.

    EXAMPLE: *What else can you expect? Who cares?*

Rhyme: Syllables or groups of syllable making the same sound.

    EXAMPLE: *whether, leather, together.*

Rhythm: In Poetry this refers to the arrangement of words into a sequence of *stressed* and *unstressed* syllables.
These are sometimes referred to as long or short syllables.

Saga: Originally this was the name given to long tales of heroes and kings from Iceland and Scandinavia – the Norse legends.
Because they frequently dealt with long family feuds the term Saga is nowadays used for any long story covering two or more family generations.

Satire: A kind of writing which exposes individuals or institutions to ridicule, usually in a comic way. It is frequently found in plays and poetry.

Second person: See under **Person**.

Semi colon: The punctuation mark (;) used to link two groups of very closely related words which could usually stand alone as sentences in their own right. Instead of using a full stop, the semi-colon is used to show a continuation of thought. The two sentences may be related in three ways.
i When the second sentence is the cause of the first.
ii When the second sentence is the result of the first.
iii When the second sentence gives more information about the first,

Study p.29

Sentence: A group of words containing a verb (either expressed or understood) and making complete sense.

Sexist language: For many years it was accepted practice to use *he* or *his* in sentences like *Each student will carry his own luggage.* even though half or more of the students might be female. Nowadays we try to avoid references to gender in such sentences by saying *All students will carry their own luggage.*

Simile: A figure of speech in which one thing is likened to another, usually from a different category.
It is usually introduced by the words *like* or *as*.   *Study p. 47*

Singular: One as opposed to **Plural** (two or more).

Slang: Words or phrases which are not an accepted part of the language.

Soliloquy: This is a speech in a play which is spoken by one of the characters, usually on stage alone, in which his or her innermost thoughts are expressed.

Sonnet: A form of poem containing fourteen lines of equal length. In English these will be of ten syllables (see **Iambic Pentameter** above) and there will be a strict rhyming pattern of *abab – cdcd – efef – gg*.

Split infinitive: The insertion of an adverb between the two words of the infinitive.

EXAMPLE: *to boldly go, to gladly accept.*

This was considered poor English, with for example, the form *boldly to go* and *to accept gladly* being more acceptable. Modern usage has led to a more tolerant attitude towards the split infinitive. *Study p.7*

Spoonerism: The mixing up of the initial letters of words, resulting in amusing misunderstandings.

EXAMPLE: *"He arrived on a well-boiled icicle"* when it should be
"...a well-oiled bicycle"

Named after Rev. W.A. Spooner (1844 – 1930) who was famous for making this kind of slip.

Subject: That part of a sentence about which something is said.

EXAMPLE: In *Harry fed the cat.* the subject is *Harry* because the sentence is about him and what he did.

(See also **Object** and **Predicate**.)

Subordinating conjunction: This is a word used to join a subordinate or dependent clause to the main clause of a sentence.
Subordinating conjunctions include such words as *because, whereas, while, until, before, after, in order to, so that, except.*

(See also **Coordinating conjunctions** above)

Suffix: letters added to the end of a word or word-root in order to modify its meaning.

EXAMPLE: *badly, kinder, kindest, hopeful, friendship.* *Study p.34/36*

Superlative: The form of adjective or adverb used to describe the third degree of comparison – **Positive** – **Comparative** – **Superlative**.

EXAMPLE: *big – bigger – biggest,*
slowly – more slowly – most slowly,
often – more often – most often.

The Comparative form may be used to compare two objects whereas the superlative is used to compare three or more. *Study p.13/16*

Synonym: A word that means the same (or almost the same) as another.

Tautology: The unnecessary repetition of the same thing in different words.
> EXAMPLE: *They arrived one after the other in succession..*
> *He died from a fatal injury.*
> *She was an unmarried spinster.*　　　　　*Study p.48*

Tense: The tense of a verb tells when the action is taking place.
The three main tenses are **Present, Past, Future**. (See above.)　*Study p.10*

Third person: See under **Person**.

Transitive verb: A verb which takes a direct object.
> EXAMPLE: *The cat killed the mouse. Michael wrote a letter.*
(see also **Intransitive verb** above and compare.)　　　*Study p.7*

Trilogy: A series of three related works such as plays or novels.

Verbosity: The use of more words than are needed.

Verb: A 'doing' word – one which indicates action, occurrence or existence:
> EXAMPLE: *walk, stood, was.*　　　　　　　*Study p.7*

Vowels: The five letters of the alphabet: *a, e, i, o u.*
Their sounds are made by vibrating the vocal cords.

Zeugma: A figure of speech in which a word (frequently a verb) is followed by two words that would not normally be found together.
The element of unexpectedness is often amusing.
> EXAMPLE: *Alice arrived in a large hat and a flood of tears.*
> *"Mr Pickwick took his hat and his leave." (Dickens.)*
>
> 　　　　　　　　　　　　　　　　　*Study p.48*

Answers

Test 1

1 **common**: drama story daughter island spirit monster arts tempest ship shores island vessel son members court brother play magic comedy butler jester play today
   proper: Tempest William Shakespeare Duke Milan Miranda Ariel Caliban Prospero King Naples Ferdinand Antonio Stephano Trinculo Shakespeare's

2 plague pride troupe crew string or stud board shoal flight litter bench

3 **masculine**: boar usher bull bachelor bridegroom peacock
   feminine: housewife hostess actress widow fiancee heiress
   common: fire-eater soldier vicar Briton duckling choir
   neuter: kingdom coffee computer traffic scissors tree

4 goodness truth happiness poverty stupidity danger religion jealousy pity mercy misery leniency success grace sadness innocence anxiety heroism courage ability

5 berries wolves mothers-in-law thieves echoes churches hobbies shelves lice passers-by cacti dwarfs heroes cities tomatoes roofs buses solos larvae stimuli

Test 2

1 a We watched the birds building their nests in the trees. b The children were given large amounts of money for their birthdays. c The fiddlers on the roofs could be wolves in sheep's clothing. d When they died we were left our aunts' houses. e They were having difficulties with the Maths tests. f There were mice in the old ladies' rooms. g Our neighbours have bought some cottages in Cornwall. h These taps' washers are worn and that is why they are dripping.

2 I wrote this sitting on a beach in Greece. I was the only person there and it was incredibly peaceful. The sun shone, the waves gently lapped the shore and from the twisted olive trees behind me there was the continuous song of the cicadas. Even as I looked a small herd of goats made their way past me and headed for the sea. Then they drank the salt water and it looked as if they were eating the pebbles. How peculiar! A large yacht sailed into the bay and the goats bleated loudly and ran away.

3 a A ball was kicked through the open window and a valuable vase was smashed.
   b The doors would be opened at nine and the auction would start at ten. c In May 1948 the State of Israel was proclaimed by the Jews. d A ban on meat from countries with foot-and-mouth disease was announced by Britain in 1967. e 'M' is played by Judi Dench in the latest 007 films. f The largest ferris wheel in the world has been constructed by engineers in London. g The recent Chess Championship was won by a seven-year-old girl. h The passive voice of the verb is often used by writers to sound less direct.

Test 3

1 **a** collapsed - intransitive, past simple tense. **b** leave and follow - both imperative and present simple tense. **c** were ... following - interrogative - past continuous tense. **d** is - present simple; to live - infinitive. **e** had been walking - past perfect continuous. **f** will have painted - future perfect.

2 saw - sawed - sawn, know - knew - known, freeze - froze - frozen, spring - sprang - sprung, cut - cut - cut, write - wrote - written, swim - swam - swum, shake - shook - shaken, rise - rose - risen, drink - drank - drunk, seek - sought - sought, speak - spoke - spoken, fight - fought - fought, ring - rang - rung, throw - threw - thrown, hurt - hurt - hurt, weave - wove - woven, tread - trod - trodden, ride - rode - ridden.

3 (There may be valid alternatives to these answers.) **a** raised **b** understand **c** telephone **d** delayed - started **e** wait - investigate **f** suffered - stop **g** collapsed - died **h** improves - enter.

Test 4

1 clear, steel-blue, all-pervading, pensive, pure, soft, robust, man-like, long, strong, lingering, snow-white, small, unspeckled, gentle, feminine, bottomless, mighty, strong, troubled, murderous, masculine.

2 **a** lovely, old, silk **b** big, Victorian, brick, town **c** small, new and blue **d** favourite, long, green, velvet **e** sweet, green, Spanish **d** nasty, heavy, black, oak, walking.

3 heroic, golden, contemptible, proud, miraculous, French, northern, tabular, scholastic, bestial.

4 chosen, suggestive, deceitful (deceptive), spoken, enchanted, lost, defensive, varied (variable), irritable, exclusive.

5 **a** The factory owner imported Welsh and German steel. **b** As well as her school job, Jane worked as a disco dancer. **c** We had a country holiday as well as a seaside one.

6 **possessive:** my, your, his, her, its, our, your (pl), their. **demonstrative:** this, that, these, those. **interrogative:** Which? What? Whose?

Test 5

1 **manner:** swiftly, relentlessly, frighteningly, carelessly, without hesitation, beautifully, gracefully, mortally. **time:** eventually, before lunchtime, soon, for several minutes, in the early morning, before sunset. **place:** at the restaurant, down the river, over the rapids, around the rocks, out of the room, on the lake, beneath his arm.

2 **a** interrogative., degree **b** probability, relative **c** frequency, degree, probability **d** probability, frequency, relative, interrogative. **e** probability (or affirmation), probability, relative, frequency **f** relative, probability, degree, probability **g** probability (or negation), frequency, degree, relative, degree, frequency, frequency.

3   **a** frequency **b** time **c** place **d** manner **e** comparative **f** superlative **g** manner - place - time.

Test 6

1
	Subject								
Subject	I	you	he	she	it		we	you (pl)	they
Object	me	you	him	her	it		us	you	them
Possessive	mine	yours	his	hers	its		ours	yours	theirs
Reflexive	myself	yourself	himself	herself	itself	ourselves	yourselves		themselves

2   **a** her ... him **b** me ... I ... them **c** him ... he ... her **d** them ... they ... us
e I ... them ... I ... they ... me **f** me ... you ... it ... him or her.

3   **a** Sylvia and I ... **b** ... Ann and me **c** You and I ... **d** Harry, Brett and I ...
e My neighbours and I ... **f** ... my sister and me.

4   **a** them ... us **b** him ... me **c** I ... him **d** We ... them **e** She, my aunt and I ...
f They .... my friends and me.

Test 7

1   **a** What **b** Who **c** What **d** Which **e** which **f** whose **g** Who **h** whom.

2   **a** This is Ann who lives .... **b** That is the castle which was lived ... **c** Ralph is a
consultant whose work ... **d** The trees are growing which will ... **e** You are the
owner to whom ... **f** Eva, with whom we are eating on Sunday, is a great cook.

3   **a** One can only be expected to do one's best. **b** None of the pictures was properly
framed. **c** No-one among the campers is allowed out after ten o'clock. **d** Each of the
twelve teams has to play two matches. **e** Few of the boys had taken their own tin-
openers. **f** If any one of you has been abroad, put up your hand.

4   **a** Any driver having an accident must report it at once. **b** The nurse on duty must sign
the form personally. **c** All pupils gaining less than 20% will have to re-sit the test.
d Volunteers must offer their services in person or they cannot be accepted. **e** Patients
must report to the desk when they see their names on the board. f: All residents are
responsible for clearing away their own rubbish. **g** Those who hesitate are lost.
h Look out for oneself.

Test 8

1   **a** She was really sad because the film had ended. **b** Jack could go swimming or he
could stay at home. **c** Although it rained a lot we still enjoyed ourselves. **d** The caller
was neither Lucy nor Aaron. **e** After I had eaten oysters I felt quite ill. **f** Lily ran down
the road but she missed the bus.

2   Coordinating conjunctions join together units of equal status while subordinating
conjunctions join subordinate or dependent clauses to the main clause of the sentence.

3   **a** with **b** on **c** among **d** of **e** to **f** about ... at ... down.

4   I crouched behind the wall opposite the Bank, my back pressed against the hard stone. Late shoppers hurried along the street, glancing at window displays, while I searched among them for Jake. Suddenly he came round the corner, ran across the street and down the hill towards me. He came to a blue door and was through it and inside the building. I raced after him and from the doorway I looked into a crowded bar. Jake was by the counter beside someone I never expected to see again.

5   **a** before - preposition, until - preposition **b** through - preposition, since - preposition, when - conjunction **c** for - preposition, since - conjunction, but - conjunction, over - adverb **d** before - preposition, and - conjunction, outside - adverb, until - conjunction **e** through - adverb, until - conjunction, across - preposition, but - conjunction, since - adverb;

Test 9

1   McRae approached the door. There was something quite forbidding about its appearance. In the distance a bell could be heard when he pulled the iron handle. Then footsteps echoed along what sounded like a stone passageway. As the door slowly creaked open McRae could hear his own heart beating. Like a cornered animal he did not know whether to stand his ground or run. Around the side of the partly opened door a head appeared. The strangest pair of eyes peered into his. At that instant he felt himself being taken into the control of something quite alien.

2   **a** It's nine o'clock and she's sure she'll be late. **b** We're wondering why we can't see what's stopping its wheels going. **c** Marie's hoping she's been chosen for the part but it isn't likely. **d** Mike's teacher collected the children's toys for the school's bazaar. **e** Mr Jones' team had to wait outside the boys' changing room. **f** James' uncle painted all the houses' front doors apart from ours. **g** Danny's dog's hurt its paw which is why it's whining. **h** I don't know what time they're arriving but they'll probably be late.

3   **a** I went out to buy nails, screws, glue, paint, wallpaper and brushes. **b** He wore a dreadful, old, baggy, green, Aran, wool, sailing pullover. **c** He said, "I'm afraid I've broken your pen." **d** You will come, wont you? **e** Following in Dad's footsteps, Joe, who is nine, wants to be a vet. **f** We are hoping, meanwhile, to do some shopping. **g** I will be flying from Madrid, Spain to Paris, France. **h** Today is Friday, 31st December, 1999.

To separate: **a** items in a list **b** list of adjectives **c** direct speech **d** question phrase at end of question **e** subordinate clauses **f** adverbs such as meanwhile, however, nevertheless **g** towns, counties, countries etc. **h** component parts of dates.

Test 10

1   **a** John said that he was going to be late for the meeting. **b** Mary whispered that she thought someone had been in there. **c** The policeman asked if Mr Smithers lived there.

d Deirdre announced that they were going to Dublin the following week. **e** The dentist ordered me to open wide so that he could have a look **f** Mrs Harris explained that I was then to go the office and say that she had sent me.

2   At a recent meeting of the Little Highton Leisure Committee, Mrs Mounce made the following speech:"Ladies and Gentlemen - fellow villagers - I am delighted to see so many of you gathered here this evening, especially when the weather is so dreadful, so thank you for making the effort. I hope you will think it worthwhile when I tell you the good news. I received a letter this very morning from the Chair of the County Council and I know you will be thrilled that he has promised to give us his full support. Furthermore we have received a cheque for £2000 from an anonymous donor, which means that there is now enough money in the fund for us to begin the first phase of the building work. I will now hand you over to Mr Jolliff who has offered to oversee the site clearance."

3   Jack said that he was extremely pleased to meet Mrs Yard, who replied that he should call her Ann as she did not think of him as a stranger. Jack told her that Harry had spoken of her often and that she had meant a great deal to him. Ann assured Jack that Harry had meant a great deal to her as well and she then asked him to tell her about it. It was why he had come, Jack replied, but now that he was there he did not find it easy. Ann begged him to tell it just as it had happened and promised that she would not interrupt. There had only been six of them left, Jack began hesitantly. He said that Harry had been his second-in-command and that he had ordered him to take two of the others and go south while the other three of them went north.

Test 11

1   **a** Ann said, "I have never known such cold weather for August." **b** "That really is a ghastly colour," Jasper remarked. **c** "The leaves are dangerous," he warned. "Take care that you do not slip." **d** "Has anyone seen my shorts?" shouted an embarrassed Arthur. **e** "Stop it!" Jack ordered. "Now stop it at once!" **f** "I bought this watch in June," she complained, "and it's never worked." **g** "This is my pen. Do you doubt it? I should think not!" he snapped. **h** Paul said he was going to Kent, adding, "Do you want to come?"

2   **a** Julie said, "On Saturday nights I like to watch 'Blind Date' and have a really hot curry." **b** "Has anyone found Mark's copy of 'The Homework Series'?" Miss Owen asked. **c** "And Elizabeth," Mr Davis announced, "will play Lady Capulet in 'Romeo and Juliet'." **d** "Humbug!" cries Scrooge in 'A Christmas Carol' by Dickens. **e** "Have you not read 'The Silver Chair'?" Katie asked. "You'll love it." **f** "Who said, 'A horse! A horse! My kingdom for a horse!'?" the questionmaster asked.

3   "What are you looking for? Ellen asked."A book!" Hugh snapped ungraciously.
"A book? What book?"
"If you must know it's 'Great Expectations'," he said. "I need it for school tomorrow."
"Where did you have it last?" she enquired.
"If I knew that I'd know where it was now," Hugh shouted.

"All right! There's no need to be rude," Ellen countered. "If you like you can borrow my copy. You did say 'Great Expectations' didn't you?"

"Yes. Thanks very much," grinned Hugh.

Test 12

1   Tel. 01569 248594

27, Hinchcliffe Gardens,
Over Hillverton,
Somerset
TA49 9GT

19th April, '00.

Greystoke Travel,
12, Coronation Avenue,
Bridgwater.

Dear Sirs,

I saw your recent advertisement for a trainee travel assistant in 'The County Gazette'. I am aged fifteen and am about to take my GCSE exams and it has always been my ambition to work in the travel industry. Although I will not be available until the middle of June I would be really pleased if you would consider me for the position.

I try to look smart and I am reliable and trustworthy, as you will see from the enclosed reference from my form teacher. My predicted grades may not be the highest but I think I can promise to make up for in hard work.

I hope to hear from you.

Yours faithfully,

John Marks.

2   The old man rolled his head. "Nay, nay, I'm past everything but dreaming, damn my bones. Don't you worry my pretty. When you've had a pain in your leg a long while it's a kind of friend." Then he added quite casually as though he were saying nothing at all:

"Georges may be riding over from Whitehaven today."

Her heart began to hammer. "Georges Paris?"

"Aye. He's grown a fine young man, but he'll burn his fingers one of these days. He's in with a lot o' rogues. I've told him, but he don't listen. Thinks he can manage them. Very confident young man is Georges."

Before she could say anything or even reason with herself about her foolish excitement Emma Furze joined them. Judith saw that she had smartened herself. She had a black hoop and a silver band in her dark hair. She looked really handsome as she stood there. There was something both foolish and good in her face; her black eyes were large and always brimming with emotion; at the slightest excuse her breast would heave and swell. She looked at Judith with a childlike smile of pleasure.

"I saw a fine man on a horse and said to myself, 'He's come to take her away.' I was tortured by the anxiety, my dear."

"You need be tortured no longer. No fine gentleman shall take me away."

Test 13

1 As fit as a fiddle   As cool as a cucumber   As dull as ditchwater
As poor as a church mouse   As sick as a dog   As flat as a pancake

As free as air   As thick as thieves   As sober as a judge
As tough as nails   She swims like a fish   He ate like a horse

2 **Similes**: shoppers …. like a hungry plague of locusts.
Metaphors: Time marches on and waits ….; the sea …. on fire, a sheet of gold;
regiments of tombstones.
Personification: the engine spluttered, coughed and died; tombstones marched; the
house waiting to welcome back its children; cliffs stood proud and defiant ….
defending; the angry sea.

Test 14

Cliches a I was told secretly that it was a matter of extreme urgency. **b** He was
unsophisticated but very generous. **c** Do not give up - a solution is within reach.
d When it was almost too late he decided to reform. **e** It is raining extremely heavily
but there is nothing in the way. **f** At the present time we should be independent. **g** As
a nation we have behaved honourably throughout history. **h** He was his mother's
favourite but he and his father were always quarrelling.

Colloquialisms a They were severe with me but I endured and showed that I had
courage. **b** We're all rather sad today because Fred has died. **c** It was their
responsibility so they will have to suffer the consequences. **d** I was doing nothing so I
took the decision and helped him. **e** This is a practical joke. You're teasing me but I'm
not fooled that easily. **f** We tried to fool him but he wasn't deceived. **g** He had spoilt
his record by falling asleep and was in disgrace. **h** Things are extremely disorganised
so let's make a start and cooperate.

Dyads high and dry, alive and kicking, Queen and Country, wear and tear, hale and
hearty, part and parcel, ready and able, through and through, wet and windy, down and
out, ins and outs, give and take.

Test 15

1 **a** She ran a shop which specialised in dresses for big women. **b** Are you an old aged
pensioner ? **c** Not only am I unwell but I am getting deaf. **d** Uncle Harry is dead.
e Her clothes were shabby and it was clear that she had no money. **f** Following an
argument with a policeman after getting drunk, he found himself in prison. **g** I think
you are telling lies. **h** As they approach old age they are going to live in an old people's
home.

2 disabled, a refuse collector, one with facial blemishes, a speech impediment, slim,
cottage in need of some renovation, vertically challenged, a portly gentleman, an
unpleasant odour.

3 **Hyperbole**: b, c, f, h.   **Litotes**: a, d, e, g.

4 **a** She was pleased to see him. **b** I waited for a very long time and became extremely bored. **c** When the firework exploded it made me start violently. **d** She liked a drink and clearly had had several. **e** Mount Everest is extremely difficult to climb. **f** Her daughter was extremely precious to her. **g** Boa constrictors are very difficult pets to look after. **h** Having run extremely fast she was very hot.

Test 16

Metonyms: **a** took up a political career, became a barrister, became a clergyman **b** The Civil Service, per person **c** the English Channel, to the Monarch **d** in credit, in debt **e** the sea **f** journalists **g** writing, war **h** the U.S. presidency.
Proverbs: **a** Don't cut off your nose to spite your face. **b** Curiosity killed the cat. **c** What can't be cured must be endured. **d** You can lead a horse to water but you can't make it drink. **e** Fair exchange is no robbery. **f** The end justifies the means. **g** All things come to those who wait. **h** He who sups with the Devil should have a long spoon. **i** March comes in like a lamb and goes out like a lion. **j** There's many a slip twixt cup and lip. **k** People in glasshouses shouldn't throw stones. **l** Red sky at night, shepherd's delight; red sky in the morning, shepherd's warning. **m** One man's drink is another man's poison. **n** A rolling stone gathers no moss. **o** Jack of all trades is master of none. **p** What's sauce for the goose is sauce for the gander. **q** A watched pot never boils. **r** One swallow does not make a summer. **s** Beauty is in the eye of the beholder.

Test 17

1 interrogative. **2** opinion > size > age > shape > colour > origin > material > purpose. (OSASCOMP). **3** imperative. **4** relative. **5** auxiliary. **6** coordinating. **7** indefinite. **8** manner, time and place. **9** infinitive. **10** comparative. **11** adverbial phrase of manner. **12** intransitive. **13** active and passive. **14** future continuous. **15** subordinating. **16** phrasal. **17** superlative. **18** interjection. **19** collective. **20** past participle. **21** frequency. **22** past perfect.

Test 18

1 alliteration. **2** assonance. **3** mixed metaphor. **4** oxymoron. **5** proverb. **6** litotes. **7** hyperbole. **8** onomatopoeia. **9** tautology. **10** cliche. **11** as or like. **12** dyads (or doubles). **13** personification. **14** irony. **15** colloquialisms. **16** euphemism. **17** metaphor.

Test 19

1 It has been said, "If you become a teacher, by your pupils you'll be taught."

2 My friend Vikram and I are hoping to become referees and if we practise hard enough we should get our licences in February. Mr Lang selected Vikram and me from twenty seven boys who applied, fewer than in previous years. When Vikram was seven, his father died. He has one brother, called Maan, but Vikram's the older. Often on Saturdays he comes round for breakfast and Mum always says, "Bacon and eggs is a good way to set you up for the day." We have a laugh but we don't say anything because Mum's really generous. She always gives us a bag of cakes to share among all of us in the team.

3   There were seven men but none of them has come forward.

4   "Please may I have a copy of 'Lord of the Flies' by William Golding?" the lady asked the bookseller.

5   Jack was lying when he said that he was lying in bed when the goose laid the golden egg.

6   The Government advised all young persons aged between fourteen and twenty definitely to register, dependent on the areas in which they lived.

7   This story takes place in the past, in days of yore, and is the tale of two boys, one the son of a baron while the other's father was a knight. One morning at the hour of eight the pair rode off to find an old manor house on the borders of Wales in which they had heard a mean, bad knave lived. A long lane led them to climb over a worn stile, through a gate, across a moat to a great red door on which they rapped with their sword. Naught but peace and quiet did they hear and then they knew their journey had been in vain.

Test 20 Crossword.

Across 1 cliche **4** phrase **7** assonance **9** mode **10** earl **11** gee **12** speech **14** rhythm **16** bathos **18** brawls **20** ill **21** lava **23** arum **24** euphemism **25** dotted **26** Daphne.
Down 1 commas **2** case **3** enough **4** player **5** race **6** emblem **7** adjective **8** earthworm **13** coo **15** her **16** ballad **17** sighed **18** blamed **19** simile **22** aunt **23** asap